Motivational Interviewing for
Working with Children and Families

Motivational Interviewing for Working with Children and Families

A PRACTICAL GUIDE FOR EARLY INTERVENTION AND CHILD PROTECTION

Donald Forrester, David Wilkins
and **Charlotte Whittaker**

Jessica Kingsley Publishers
London and Philadelphia

First published in Great Britain in 2021 by Jessica Kingsley Publishers
An Hachette Company

5

Copyright © Donald Forrester, David Wilkins and Charlotte Whittaker 2021

A CIP catalogue record for this title is available from the
British Library and the Library of Congress

ISBN 978 1 78775 408 9
eISBN 978 1 78775 409 6

Printed and bound by CPI Group (UK) Ltd, Croydon, CR0 4YY

Jessica Kingsley Publishers' policy is to use papers that are natural, renewable and recyclable
products and made from wood grown in sustainable forests. The logging and manufacturing
processes are expected to conform to the environmental regulations of the country of origin.

Jessica Kingsley Publishers
Carmelite House
50 Victoria Embankment
London EC4Y 0DZ

www.jkp.com

For our children
Hannah, Ruth and James
Isabelle, Finley and Taylor
and
Maeve

Contents

Part One: What is motivational interviewing?

Part Two: How can we use motivational interviewing in child and family work?

Part Three: How can we become good at MI?

Acknowledgements

We owe so much to so many people that acknowledging them all seems impossible. Here we can only identify a few of those who have helped us in developing our thinking and practice around motivational interviewing and social work. We have learnt so much from the wisdom of Bill Miller and Steve Rollnick – who have been unstintingly encouraging and supportive and generous. The whole MI community has been welcoming and thought-provoking and helpful at every stage. Too many have contributed to name each one individually, but the warmth of the community and its commitment to constantly learning are some of the things we love about MI.

We are also incredibly lucky to have worked with hundreds of fantastic social workers, so many of whom embraced learning MI and allowed us to indulge our curiosity by observing, recording and thinking about their practice. This includes workers from many local authorities, but we are particularly indebted to Islington, where we had researchers embedded in teams for several years and developed firm friendships and had lots of fun as well as learning a lot about social work. In a similar vein, we are grateful to have been able to embed MI into the heart of the Frontline social work course, and learnt as much from doing so as the students we worked with. We hope that for both groups this book will help answer some of the endless thought-provoking questions you asked! We would also like to thank people who read chapters of the book or chapters that did not eventually make it in, including Lucy Sheehan, Dan Burrows and Lucy Allison.

Finally, we are all fortunate enough to work or study in the CASCADE Centre for Children's Social Care at Cardiff University and we want to thank our colleagues there for providing such a supportive, curious and kind place to think about social work. We are particularly grateful to Aimee Grant for looking over and improving a final draft of the book.

Donald, David and Charlie

A note on using real meetings

An important feature of this book is that most of the examples we use are real social workers meeting parents which we recorded as part of research studies. We believe that this makes the book far richer and closer to practice than it would be if it was based on made-up or imagined meetings (Hall and White 2005). Here we just wanted to clarify the situation in relation to the examples we use.

Most of the examples we used were meetings between parents and social workers. Some were meetings between a social worker and an actor playing a parent. These are called 'simulated interviews'. Simulated interviews can be useful for seeing how different social workers approach the same meeting. For instance, in Chapters 5 and 6 we present very different approaches to the same scenario – with real meetings it is not possible to see how it might have gone differently.

We had consent to use the recordings we made from both workers and parents and, in a few instances and when appropriate, young people. We have changed or left out any potential identifying details, so all presented interactions are anonymised.

Although we have tried to use real examples, this has not always been possible. So we have also imagined parts of conversations. These are usually short interchanges to demonstrate a particular point. We have also used a few case study examples from our practice experience. These have been changed so that no family or individual could be identified from them.

As most of our examples are based on real interviews, we do not always specify this in the text – real interviews are the default. Where it is a simulated interview or an imagined interchange, we indicate this in the text.

Introduction

This book is concerned with one apparently simple but actually very complicated question: how can we talk to people in helpful ways? And, in particular, how can we have helpful conversations in the context of child and family social work, when there might be serious concerns about a child's safety?

Our motivation for writing the book comes from two sets of experiences. We have all worked in frontline child protection work. We experienced the enormous challenges of the work, as well as the sense of satisfaction when we did help a child or a family. Yet we felt that too often we were not helping people – we were trying to, but did not have a clear theory and practice for making a difference.

We then moved into teaching and research, and our second motivation was discovering that we were not alone. Not having a clear sense of how to do the work, or why to do it in particular ways, was normal. There was widespread hunger for better guidance on how to do this incredibly difficult job.

In particular, there was remarkably little detailed consideration of how to have difficult conversations, such as ones in which you have to raise serious concerns. Many social work theories agree that relationships between workers and parents and children are incredibly important, yet they tend to provide limited guidance on how to develop such relationships in this context. A particularly important challenge is that most of these ideas are borrowed from therapeutic conversations. There seemed to be much less written about how to have difficult conversations – how to raise serious concerns or explain you are going to take action such as starting care proceedings. Yet this type of conversation was the bread and butter of our practice experience. To be useful, it seems to us, any approach to communication in this context has to help us have these conversations in a more constructive way.

In trying to understand better how to do this central element of the work, we were drawn to motivational interviewing. Three things attracted us. First, the values of respect and empathy were consistent with those that brought us into this work. As we discuss in the next chapter, motivational interviewing comes from a humanist perspective that has made many of the most important contributions to how we can understand and help people. Its values, theoretical orientation and theories are a good fit for social work.

Second, motivational interviewing provides a detailed description of why change is often difficult and how we can help people to change difficult behaviours. In particular, a central concern was understanding and working with 'resistance' – which can be any form of non-cooperation, from threats to responding passively in a conversation. This seemed a really helpful focus for any approach in social work with children and their families, because a high proportion of families are resistant to the involvement of statutory child protection services. Motivational interviewing helps us understand why and makes suggestions for what we can do about it.

Finally, motivational interviewing has a strong evidence base – indeed, it has had many hundreds of studies. This is important because the evidence base suggests that motivational interviewing tends to work: people find it helpful and it is particularly good for engaging people in services. We are less confident that some other popular approaches in social work have this sort of evidence base. Yet this evidence does not simply tell us that it 'works'. Just as importantly, it helps us understand its limitations. Motivational interviewing does not claim to be some sort of magic wand that can always create change. It is a detailed, evidence-based and ethical theory that describes key practices that make change more likely.

Motivational interviewing was not developed for child and family work. It originated in working with alcohol problems and has been used with a wide variety of behaviour-change issues. It was then adapted to situations where the helper has a position of power, such as a probation or prison officer. We have researched motivational interviewing in child and family work extensively over the last 20 years and tried to think about how it can be used and adapted for this setting.

This book is an attempt to share our learning from practice, research and teaching hundreds of people motivational interviewing over the last 20 years. Throughout, we have tried to make most of the examples relate to the realities of practice in children's services (although sometimes it has been useful to consider what a counsellor might say in a similar situation). In particular, we are fortunate to have recorded a lot of conversations in which workers meet parents and young people. This book benefits from using real examples of social workers having these conversations throughout; as discussed in the note at the beginning, extracts are anonymised and used with the consent of those who took part. We hope that being able to read how real social workers dealt with often difficult conversations will bring the book to life for you, and make thinking about how to apply the skills feel more real and grounded in practice.

Overview of the book

The book is divided into three main parts.

Part One – What is motivational interviewing?

Part One consists of five chapters which provide a basic introduction to what motivational interviewing is and how to do it. Throughout, we use examples from child and family work; however, the principles and skills we discuss are ones that apply across different settings. Chapter 1 considers the background to MI, setting it in the broader context of humanist psychology and describing the historical development of the approach. Chapter 2 considers core concepts and principles within MI, including the theory of change that underpins the method – in other words, trying to understand why people struggle to change problem behaviours and how we can best help them. Chapter 3 introduces core skills, such as open questions, affirmations and reflections. Chapter 4 discusses how we can manage an interview overall and the different stages of an MI interview, and considers the final key skill – summary statements. In Chapter 5 we present approaches to giving advice and information from an MI perspective, both because this is an important part of everyday practice and also because it allows us to introduce key concepts for child and family work such as directiveness and dialogue.

Part Two – How can we use motivational interviewing in child and family work?

Part Two considers how we might apply the principles and skills involved in motivational interviewing to the challenging task of child protection work. It goes beyond the basics of motivational interviewing and shares our understanding of how motivational interviewing principles and skills can be used to have difficult conversations. Chapter 6 considers what good authority is and how we might use it. It is centrally concerned with how to direct a conversation and raise difficult issues in a respectful spirit, while acknowledging the other person's views. Chapter 7 develops these ideas further. It articulates the concept of 'purposeful dialogue' as being central to good practice and outlines how motivational interviewing can allow us to achieve such dialogues. It ends with a very difficult case example, to explore ways in which motivational interviewing can be used across the spectrum of child and family work. Chapter 8 focuses on how we can use the principles of motivational interviewing to work with children and young people, considering insights for direct work and the use of motivational interviewing to help children change behaviour. A central concern of this chapter is to explore the limits of motivational interviewing in working with children in this setting.

Part Three – How can we become good at MI?

The final part of the book considers how you might improve your own practice and those of others. Chapter 9 sets out ways you can improve your skills and understanding of MI. It introduces the idea of recording and coding your own practice and provides some suggestions for doing this. Chapter 10 reviews ways in which you might help others become good at MI, including through training, supervision and observing and feeding back on practice.

Finally, in Chapter 11 we reflect on key issues arising from the book and offer suggestions for future directions for the development of motivational interviewing in child and family work.

PART ONE

WHAT IS MOTIVATIONAL INTERVIEWING?

Chapter 1

What is motivational interviewing?

AND WHY MIGHT IT BE HELPFUL FOR WORKING WITH CHILDREN AND THEIR FAMILIES?

Chapter overview

This chapter considers what motivational interviewing is and why it may be a helpful approach for social workers and other professionals working with children and their families. It provides a brief history of motivational interviewing, locating it within a broader tradition of humanist psychology and social work. More recent developments in motivational interviewing and its uses for work with children and families where there are child protection concerns are considered. The chapter then outlines the structure for the rest of the book.

Introduction

Imagine you are visiting a woman because the school has made a referral that she seems to be drunk when picking up her five-year-old child. In addition, the child often seems dirty and is sometimes not dressed appropriately for the weather. There is a history of concerns around alcohol use by this woman – let's call her Jeanette. You meet with her to talk about these concerns. What should you say and how should you say it?

This is the type of conversation that social workers have every day with parents and carers, yet such conversations are really difficult, and workers often struggle with how to manage such challenging meetings. Helping people who think they have a problem is hard enough. The whole field of counselling is built around how to do that well. Yet a moment's consideration suggests that the type of conversation we are thinking about is much more difficult than a counselling meeting. On the face of it, it seems likely that Jeanette may have an alcohol problem which is affecting her ability to care for her child. Yet it is also likely there will be other elements of the situation that we are not aware of. Perhaps she is depressed, or living in poverty, has problems at work or in her own relationships. Maybe she has had contact with social workers in the past and not had a very good experience. Jeanette may or may not consider that her use of alcohol is a problem for her or for her child.

Even if drinking is the primary issue, in practice it is unlikely that Jeanette will simply open up and say so during a first encounter with a child and family social worker. Jeanette is very likely to deny or minimise the problem. And if so, this would be an understandable and even rational response. While minimisation and denial are common in counselling, the statutory nature of child and family social work, particularly with the possibility – however remote – of a child being removed, makes it even more likely and understandable. Thus, the professional has the complex task of raising concerns, offering opportunities for Jeanette to give her opinion, and from there beginning to assess the needs and risks for the child and think about how best to help. How on earth do workers do this? And how should they? It seems almost impossibly difficult – yet child and family social workers are doing it, every day of the week (and at weekends too!). In Chapters 6 and 7 we examine how different social workers approached working with a parent like Jeanette.

This takes us to the central question that this book is concerned with, namely: what is good practice with children and families where there are concerns about a child's welfare? How should workers have difficult conversations such as this in ways that are both ethical and effective? And how can MI help us do this complicated work better?

While social workers spend a comparatively small amount of their time in direct contact with parents and children, we believe this contact is the most important part of the social work role. It is the time when we build relationships, assess need and risk, and try to help people change. Historically, it has always been thought of as the time when the 'magic happens'. The desire to help people is overwhelmingly the main motivation for people entering social work (Csikai and Rozensky 1997), and the sense that we are making a difference is probably the main reason why people stay in such work. Yet *how* do social workers help people? What is 'the magic' of helping? Despite the central importance of this issue, for many years social work researchers and practice leaders have primarily focused on other aspects of the role or the wider organisation – and so, although there is a widespread expectation that social workers will help people via direct practice, there is little published research that explicitly describes how. This is where motivational interviewing may be useful.

Motivational interviewing – usually referred to as MI from now on – is a theoretically sophisticated approach to helping that has a strong evidence base in other settings, including health care, rehabilitation, public health, dentistry, coaching and education (Miller and Moyers 2017). There is also good evidence that it can be helpful in child protection or similar settings (Forrester *et al.* 2008c, 2018, 2019). Of particular importance is the fact that understanding and working with client resistance is a central element of MI (think of Jeanette's denial (at least initially) that she has a problem and how to work with that). This is not true of all counselling or therapeutic approaches, most of which assume that people want help and then outline ways of providing it. That is often not the case in social work and is particularly unlikely to be the case in child protection situations. Here, resistance is a ubiquitous feature of practice. One of the features of MI that makes it a good fit for social work is that resistance is a central concept. The strength of the evidence base is also important. There have been thousands of studies of MI, including many with children and families, and this helps us know not just whether it works but also why it works and with whom it works best – as well as when it does not work so well.

To provide some context and understand in greater depth why MI may be a good 'fit' for child and family work, it is worth knowing a bit about how MI developed, before considering how applicable it might be for child and family social work and the different ways in which the practitioner might use it.

A brief history of MI

MI was initially developed in the field of alcohol treatment in the early 1980s. The first key papers were written by William R. Miller, a psychologist working in New Mexico. His ideas resonated with Stephen Rollnick, who was practising as a psychologist in the UK. Together, they have written the key book – now in its fourth edition – and provided much of the initial research and theorising around MI (Miller and Rollnick 2013). The ideas of MI have resonated with many and there is now a large community and body of research focused on developing MI still further.

To appreciate the revolutionary nature of MI in the alcohol field at that time, it is necessary to understand some of the context. Much treatment for alcohol problems at the time focused on alcoholism as a disease. Denial and minimisation were seen as symptoms of this disease, and it was common for professionals to use very confrontational approaches. This might include 'interventions' where families and others gather around and confront an individual with their problem in a structured and challenging meeting, or residential units with forms of individual or group confrontation. There also tended to be a focus on abstinence – not drinking at all – as the primary goal for any treatment, and little interest in the people with the alcohol problem deciding what goals they wanted to achieve.

During the 1980s and beyond, approaches to helping people with alcohol problems that challenged this orthodoxy emerged. MI was perhaps the most influential of these, but it was not alone. These included the development of the transtheoretical theory of change (Proschaska and DiClemente 1984), a focus on the impact of brief interventions and interest in more evidence-based methods (Bien *et al.* 1993). The time was perhaps ripe for exploration of more effective and less confrontational ways of working with people – a contextual development that contemporary children's services perhaps shares with the alcohol field then.

Miller developed his thinking about how to help people when he had to explain why he did what he did in helping people with alcohol problems during a series of seminars with psychologists in Norway. This led to the first paper outlining some of the key principles of MI (Miller 1983). While MI has been developed and elaborated significantly since then, the key focus on client-centred relationships and evoking intrinsic motivation remain (don't worry if these two terms are new to you, as we discuss them in more detail later on in the book).

The development of MI as something of an antidote to excessively confrontational approaches is probably a key element in its success. It has often been used in situations where previously there has been a tendency to tell people what to do – particularly when services find that telling people what to do rarely worked! Thus, MI was used in all sorts of behaviour-change situations, from helping people eat more vegetables to giving up heroin. This is obviously one of the attractions of MI for child protection work. When there are concerns about a child, it is easy to find ourselves telling parents what their problems are and what they need to do about them. In fact, we have heard this many times in meetings between social workers and parents. One problem with this approach, quite aside from a lack of effectiveness, is that it often leads to (even) more difficult conversations, which sound more like arguments than ways of helping. The promise of MI is that it offers a more constructive way to have these potentially difficult conversations and is also more likely to lead to change than simply telling people what to do.

A wider history

It is important and probably helpful to understand MI as part of a broader tradition. Miller is the first to emphasise that his approach to practice did not simply pop into his head. MI is to a large degree based on the work of Carl Rogers and his concept of person-centred counselling (Rogers 1951). In the next two chapters we outline person-centred counselling in some detail, and then consider the ways in which MI builds on the approach. Here, we want to think about the broader tradition that both MI and person-centred counselling are a part of, namely humanist psychology. Humanist psychology arose predominantly in the USA in the years following the Second World War. It has also been enormously influential in social work. Early psychology was dominated by two traditions, and humanist psychology arose in large part in opposition to these.

The first of the existing traditions was Freudianism, and the psychodynamic approach more generally. This emphasised intrinsic motivation for human behaviour, with an emphasis on primal drives. Freud's theory posited two fundamental drives – Eros and Thanatos (Galdston 1955). Eros is essentially the drive for sex, Thanatos the drive to self-destruction. Freudian theory included a sophisticated account of how these primal drives are controlled and sublimated, within the individual and by society. Freudians developed concepts, such as the unconscious (emotions we have but do not have conscious access to) that we take for granted today. A key preoccupation was understanding how and why people who were seeking help seemed to find addressing problems difficult. Through deep consideration of internal resistance to change, Freudians developed the foundations for what we now understand as counselling, as well as key elements of child development. For instance, attachment theory was developed in large part from Freudian concepts and ideas.

The other tradition in psychology was behaviourism. Initially developed by Pavlov and others, behaviourism was built through the work of Skinner and colleagues before and after the Second World War (Wozniak 1993). In contrast to Freudians, behaviourists emphasise extrinsic motivations and specifically the ways in which rewards and punishments can and do shape animal and human behaviour.

Freudianism and behaviourism provide as stark a contrast in their images of humanity as it is possible to imagine. In one, drives come from within; in the other, we are shaped by our environment. One emphasises our internal world and emotions, the other solely observable behaviour. One rejects the scientific method; the other is built entirely on it. Yet, while the contrasts are stark, to the modern eye they share one key feature: both seem to us rather bleak views of human nature. One can speculate that perhaps they are products of their time – the late 19th and early 20th centuries were characterised by human brutality on an almost unprecedented scale. Regardless of the reasons for their rather negative view of human beings, in opposition to these traditions humanist psychology developed a more positive view.

Humanist psychology sees humans as agents of their own destiny, driven by an innate desire for personal growth and fulfilment (Grassi 2000). It celebrates the positive side of human nature, such as sustaining relationships and making a helpful contribution to society. It is, in comparison to Freudian or behaviourist approaches, a very upbeat vision of humans and our societies. One example of a humanist approach is Maslow's hierarchy of need (Maslow 1954), which was developed to move beyond Freudian and behaviourist conceptions of what motivates us. Maslow prioritised needs from the most basic (air to breathe) through to the highly abstract (the drive to self-actualise – in other words, to become the best person we can be). Another example of a humanist approach is that of Erikson, who developed a theory about human change across the life course (Erikson 1959), rather than focusing solely on early childhood as Freudians tend to. He thereby popularised ideas such as the adolescent identity or the mid-life crisis, which he considered to be both crises and opportunities for reflection and growth. In more recent years the broad range of strengths-based and solution-focused approaches have all developed from the humanist tradition, with a positive view of human beings and our potential for change.

Carl Rogers was a key theorist within the humanist tradition. He believed that people have the ability to provide their own solutions to difficulties that they have. As such, the goal of the counsellor was primarily to hold a mirror up to the person so that they could find their own answers, within the context of a caring and respectful relationship. MI was built on this foundation.

What should begin to be apparent is that how we think about how to help people is not a simple, technical issue, such as finding out what works. Different approaches have implicit or explicit assumptions about human nature, the helping relationship and often what a good society might look like. MI is no exception, and one of our contentions is that some of the challenges we experience as practitioners in doing MI are that we are often struggling with these broader issues – even if we do not realise it. For instance, to return to the example of Jeanette, a Freudian, a behaviourist and an MI-influenced humanist worker would all approach how to have such conversations very differently. So, indeed, would a worker who did not use any particular approach. In developing a specific approach to our work, we are not just learning some useful tools; rather, we are embracing a wider way of thinking about the nature of problems and how helping might work.

Contemporary developments in MI

We outline what MI involves in detail with practice examples in the next few chapters. Here, we provide a high-level overview of the key insights provided by MI and how it has been used and developed over the years. As already noted, Miller started from the principles of Rogerian counselling which emphasises non-directive and client-centred listening. However, his experience in counselling people was that if his listening was genuinely non-directive – that is, he was just seeking to reflect back to people an understanding of their situation – people with alcohol problems would sometimes not make much progress, either within conversations or their lives more generally. Their talk might begin to have a repetitive quality; they were stuck, and listening carefully made it more apparent that they were stuck, but often did not help resolve the sense of 'stuckness'.

From this arose two key insights for MI. First, the level of resistance clients expressed was minimal when they were listened to in a non-judgemental way. This was a surprise, as often resistance was characterised as a feature of 'alcoholism'. It suggested that resistance – including denial and minimisation – was not a product of the individual with the alcohol problem, but of the nature of the discussion between the individual and the helper. When the helper adopted a confrontational approach, resistance increased. When the helper listened attentively and adopted a non-judgemental approach, resistance decreased (Miller and Mount 2001; Patterson and Forgatch 2001; Glynn and Moyers 2010). As a result, MI emphasises the importance of good listening skills to minimise client resistance. We return to this key idea in more detail in Chapter 2.

The second insight was that people with alcohol problems often felt ambivalent. On the one hand, they could see that their drinking was causing them and other people a range of problems. On the other hand, they might value some things about drinking or doubt their ability to stop – or both. MI developed ways of understanding and helping people resolve this ambivalence. Crucially, in doing so MI moved from non-directive listening to a directive form of client-centred conversation. Specifically, when using MI in the context of problem drinking, the aim – the direction of the discussion – is to help people resolve ambivalence and, if they wish to, move to address their alcohol misuse.

Miller combined obvious skills as a counsellor with a rigorous approach to research (Miller and Moyers 2017). Over the decades that followed, he carried out numerous studies. Initially, the results were extremely promising: even very brief MI interventions seemed able to help people address their drinking in a way that conventional approaches such as giving advice or telling people what to do could not. This initial work inspired many other researchers, and there is now an enormous body of research on MI, including hundreds of randomised controlled trials (RCTs) – the most robust test of whether something works. Here we highlight some of the key developments and findings from this body of work.

First, in the field of alcohol treatment MI achieved fairly consistently positive results. Most strikingly in two very big and influential trials, one in the US (Group 1993, 1997, 1998) and one in the UK (Team 2005), brief MI-based help of three or four sessions was as effective as much more intensive and longer interventions, including weekly sessions over months. MI has been so consistently effective that it has become to some degree the 'industry standard'; the evidence for MI is so extensive that other approaches need to show they can do as well or better than it. This is not to say that MI will be suitable for everyone. Many people benefit from group-based and service-user-led programmes such as Alcoholics Anonymous. For some people, other approaches may be better – for example, individuals with more entrenched alcohol problems usually require more than MI. However, even for these groups the MI style of communication is usually an element of the overall approach. Put simply, MI has succeeded in replacing to a large degree the confrontational or expert-led approach that dominated previously. Perhaps, we wonder, might it usefully do something similar in children's services?

Given the success of MI in working with alcohol problems, there have been extensive attempts to adapt MI for different settings. Miller's collaborator Stephen Rollnick has been a key driver in these innovations. Rollnick and others have adapted the principles of MI conversations for use in a range of settings. As a result, MI has resonated with professionals in a wide variety of practice contexts. It has been adapted and used by prison officers, psychologists, GPs, nurses, coaches and non-professional volunteers, and been used to address issues as diverse as offending behaviour, healthy eating, medication adherence, anxiety disorders, depression, sexual health and exercise. A common feature of attempts to use MI is that often the conventional approach to behaviour change in a particular context has been ineffective. For instance, exhortations to eat more healthily and telling people their drug use will kill them so often seem to fall on deaf ears. In these contexts, MI seems more effective.

In more recent years, there has been a focus on combining MI with other methods. In doing so, MI is seen as making a particular contribution to engaging people and helping them get ready to change behaviour, while other methods may be used once people feel that they want to change. Thus, for instance, MI has been combined with cognitive behavioural therapy to address anxiety disorders (Randall and McNeil 2017), or found to make perpetrators of domestic abuse more likely to engage with treatment (Musser *et al.* 2008). Simultaneously, Rollnick and others have been exploring applications of the principles of MI in even more contexts, such as within the field of educational provision (Rollnick *et al.* 2016).

A few features of these varied developments are worthy of comment. One is that across the hundreds of RCTs that have been carried out, MI is often more effective than other approaches, and even if it is equally effective, it often seems to achieve the desired effect more quickly than other comparable interventions (Lundahl *et al.* 2010). Strikingly, there seems to be little evidence that MI produces worse outcomes than a comparison treatment. This is rather surprising – with so many studies, you would think some might produce a negative outcome. Yet something about the gentle nature of MI seems to mean it rarely does any harm. Given that doing no harm should be a central principle for social work involvement with children and families, this finding seems very important.

Second, the principles of MI resonate with a wide range of professions confronted with an extraordinary array of behaviour-change issues. There seems to be something about the insights into behaviour change and practical ways of supporting it that people find helpful across a remarkably wide range of issues.

Third, this leads to interesting questions about what MI actually is. Is it simply a technique that can be used to help around specific behaviour change issues? Or is it a broader set of principles that allow us to think about how to understand and help people better? We return to this question in the final chapter, by which time you should have a good grounding in MI. We tend towards the latter position and aim to make the argument so compelling that, by the final chapter, you will too.

⏸ PAUSE AND CONSIDER...

We have presented the background to the development of MI. You might want to think about these questions:

- Do you see parallels between the previous tendency of alcohol treatment to tell people what changes they need to make and elements of current practice in child and family services?

- What do you think would be the positives about using an approach such as MI in work with children and families?

- What might be some of the key challenges or limitations?

MI with children and families

The development and use of MI in social work with children and families is comparatively recent and so the evidence that it helps and does no harm is by necessity far more limited. This is complicated by the fact that MI is often incorporated as just one element of a broader approach to helping families. Nonetheless, there is now a convincing body of research to suggest MI can be useful in working with children and families, particularly when there are serious child protection issues to be addressed.

The earliest published uses of MI in child protection work saw it integrated into services that provide holistic interventions for children at high risk of entering care. For instance, an intensive family preservation service in Wales (called 'Option 2') used MI as a foundational communication style in a service that was based on crisis intervention to prevent children coming into care. Option 2 showed evidence that it was effective and parents commented on it very positively – particularly compared with their experiences of 'normal' child protection work (Forrester *et al.* 2008a). The findings from these evaluations led to specialist Intensive Family Support Teams being rolled out across Wales, with MI as a core element in the way they worked.

A second important service that uses an MI approach is the Family Drug and Alcohol Courts (FDAC). Where care proceedings have been started and a parent has a drug or alcohol problem, FDAC has been shown to keep a higher proportion of children at home (Harwin *et al.* 2014; Zhang *et al.* 2019). FDAC has many elements, but MI is the basic communication style used in the team supporting parents. Again, it would appear that MI makes an important contribution to a complex intervention that helps families where there are serious child protection concerns.

In a review for the Scottish Government of social work services for substance misuse, Galvani and Forrester (2011) found that MI was often a key element of specialist services for children and families. In addition to Option 2 and FDAC, it was, for instance, incorporated into intensive case management and 'Recovery Coach Services'.

In recent years, there has been increasing interest in MI as a foundational communication style for child and family social workers more generally, and there is an appetite to use MI in children's services. This is in part because local authorities are moving to develop models of good practice. The norm used to be that services would often let workers get on with working out how they want to practise. Today there is more focus on developing and supporting specific practice models. This allows services to think about what training they want to deliver but also how staff can be selected and supported to deliver high-quality practice. A practice model – whether it is Signs of Safety, Restorative Practice or MI – can therefore provide a useful guide to build a service around.

The Family Safeguarding model developed in Hertfordshire incorporated MI as a central element of a model that strived to provide better support for families across the whole of children's services. This was supplemented by specialist adult workers coming into teams and other innovations. The early signs were encouraging, with workers embracing the new approach and fewer children entering care (Forrester *et al.* 2017). As a result, at the time of writing, the Family Safeguarding model is being rolled out across six more local authorities (Cambridgeshire, Lancashire, Swindon, Telford and Wrekin, Walsall, Wandsworth) – with MI training being provided for large numbers of social workers.

Islington Children's Services have also been committed to developing MI-based practice for almost ten years now. Initiatives have included extensive training, coaching and feedback for workers and supervisors alike (Luckock *et al.* 2017). Results from these studies inform several of the subsequent chapters, particularly Chapters 9 and 10. As a result of these examples, more and more local authorities in the UK are trying out MI as part of their approach to improving practice.

Conclusion

MI seems a particularly promising approach for use in work with children and families:

- The person-centred values of MI are consistent with social work principles.

- The practices of MI, and particularly the focus on understanding and working with resistance, seem a good fit with the challenges social workers often face.

- The evidence base for MI is strong, and this allows us to have a deep understanding of what does and does not work in relation to MI.

The next chapter introduces key concepts within MI, before Chapters 3 and 4 consider the key skills and how to use them in interviews.

Chapter 2

How to help people

Chapter overview

This chapter outlines key principles within MI. It introduces the crucial concept of ambivalence about change as a barrier to helping people, and considers what 'motivation' is. The ideas of 'resistance', 'sustain talk' and its conceptual opposite, 'change talk', are then considered. Taken together, motivation, ambivalence, resistance and change talk are the foundations for understanding MI. They provide a high-level description of both how we can help people change and goals for our practice that inform and justify the skills outlined in future chapters. We then turn to consider the additional complexities of these concepts as applied in a social work setting, and provide examples drawn from real meetings between workers and parents to describe and analyse resistance, change talk and ambivalence.

How do we help people?

While all social workers and related professionals share a desire to help people, there is often a lack of clarity about how they might achieve this. Sometimes workers can provide practical help. People may need assistance in getting support from a charity or other agency, such as housing. These are important ways of helping people that can make a real difference. Yet they are usually only a small part of the help that a social worker can offer. For most of this book, we are concerned with how social workers can help or hinder people through the way they talk to them about their difficulties.

Surprisingly, when we ask social work students – and even sometimes qualified workers – how they think they help people, they find it remarkably difficult to answer. There is a sense that a warm and respectful relationship is important, but this is hardly a theory for how we might help people. It is worth asking: *how* does a good relationship help people? There are some accounts we find rather unconvincing – for instance, that the relationship with the social worker can in some way provide a model of positive relationships for people who have had poor relationships in early life. In our research, we found that while worker skills could build a positive relationship, on its own a positive relationship did not help families achieve their goals (Forrester *et al.* 2019). What was needed was a relationship directed to a purpose – that purpose being to collaboratively create change for a child. Seen like this, MI provides a description of both how to build a relationship and how to ensure that the relationship is purposeful and likely to be helpful.

If the quality of the relationship is not always enough on its own, what else is needed? Here we feel MI has important insights to support a relationship-based approach to helping people. To really understand why a particular approach is helpful for people, we need a theory of helping. A theory of helping characterises the nature of the problems being worked with, explains why change may be difficult, and offers ways to be helpful. Central to MI's theory of helping are the related concepts of motivation and ambivalence.

Ambivalence

In broad terms, MI thinks of people's readiness to change in relation to any given issue as being on a spectrum. At one end of the spectrum might be 'no desire to change' and at the other end 'ready, willing and able to change'. This spectrum of readiness to change has a profound influence on whether one needs help, and the type of conversations that might be helpful. For instance, consider the five stages of change as described in the transtheoretical model in Table 2.1 (Proschaska and DiClemente 1984). The transtheoretical model of change was developed independently of MI, but it usefully helps us identify that people's attitude towards behaviour change may vary.

Now think about how ready *you* currently feel in relation to the following potential behaviour-change issues:

- eating more healthily

- using your mobile phone less

- stopping your use of single use plastic.

Table 2.1   Five-point transtheoretical model of change

Precontemplation (not ready)	Contemplation (getting ready)	Preparation (ready)	Action	Maintenance
No intention to change in the foreseeable future (within the next 6 months)	Intention to change within the foreseeable future, but acutely aware of the pros and cons of doing so	Intention to change within the immediate future (within one month), with a plan of action in mind	Change has already taken place (within the past 6 months)	Working to prevent relapse (reverting to previous behaviour)

You may find yourself at different points on the scale for each of these different issues. With a bit more thought, you can probably identify other changes that you feel more or less predisposed to making.

There are three key points to make about this scale. The first is that typically people at each end need relatively little professional help. If somebody really does not think they have a problem, and they definitely do not want to change, then usually professional involvement is likely to be limited. Such people are unlikely to go to, or remain in, counselling. At the other end of the scale, people who feel they want to make a change and believe they are able to make that change also do not usually require much professional input. Evidence suggests that even for people with fairly serious problems – very heavy drinking, for example – where motivation is high, people will often make substantial changes without professional involvement (Burman 1997).

The second point is that typically, then, professionals are involved with people who are somewhere in the middle of this scale – what the transtheoretical model calls the contemplation and preparation stages. The person, or someone else, thinks there is a problem and although there may be some desire to change, there are also good reasons for not changing. For example, a parent might be contemplating leaving an abusive relationship. They might want things to be better for their children and to end a pattern of abuse they too experienced as a child. They might also be worried about how they will cope practically and financially, and whether their children will resent them in the future. They may have a well-founded fear of the consequences of leaving.

The bulk of professional helping is with people who are somewhere near the middle of this scale. They see some reasons for changing, and have some motivation to do so, but there are also powerful reasons for not doing so. MI characterises this as *ambivalence*. At the heart of MI is working with people to resolve ambivalence. This can be a powerful way of helping facilitate behaviour change, although, as with any help, there is always the possibility that someone might decide not to change. Deciding not to change is certainly one way of resolving ambivalence, albeit one that may have some negative consequences, especially when child protection professionals are involved.

The concept of ambivalence as a key challenge for behaviour change is a core principle of MI. Resolving ambivalence can increase motivation, but it also recognises and supports individual self-determination. Self-determination is one of the foundational principles of social work – the sense that we should be helping people to have as much control over their lives as possible (Plant 2009). In so far as MI supports self-determination through support to resolve ambivalence, it is consistent with this social work value. Indeed, a focus on self-determination shapes the whole approach to working with people outlined in this book.

The third point to make is that people's attitudes towards change are shaped by many factors. Most of us would probably agree that we should exercise more, use our phones less and reduce our use of plastic. Yet our readiness to change our current behaviour is influenced by our social and economic circumstances and any or all of the following:

- personal and political beliefs and feelings
- current behaviour and perceptions of the harm it causes
- enjoyment of the behaviour
- confidence in our ability to change
- the importance this issue has for us
- responsibilities for others
- family and community perceptions of the issue
- resources and options available to support change.

Helping people to explore and resolve ambivalence is therefore likely to involve consideration of many issues on multiple levels. It involves talking about personal values and goals, and these are usually shaped and influenced by family, friends, experiences and many other factors. Thus, while the theory of change within MI is relatively simple, the practice needs to be able to embrace great complexity.

Ambivalence and motivation

Ambivalence and how to engage with it is a key issue for counselling situations. It is also clear that it is important in many other professional conversations, such as those between doctors and patients. Ambivalence too is a common feature in child protection practice. Almost all parents want the best for their children. The context of child protection may make explicit the ways in which a parent is not doing the best by their child. In fact, for most parents most of the time – not just those a social worker is working with – there is a space between how they are behaving and the sort of parent that they would like to be. For a parent where there are social work concerns, this space is likely to be greater, as there are identified problems for the child.

This gap is how we characterise *motivation*. Motivation is driven by a perceived gap between who we want to be, how we want to behave and our current behaviour. Often this takes us to our core values – what sort of person do we want to be? What sort of parent would we like to be? And what sort of parent are we being at the moment? Identifying and working with this 'motivational gap' is at the heart of good practice using MI. MI is an opportunity for people to explore whether this gap exists, and, if it does, what they would like to do about it. Where there is not a gap, there is unlikely to be motivation to change. If we are happy with how we eat or exercise or look after our child, if we are meeting our hopes and expectations, then we are not going to change our eating, exercise or parenting behaviour. MI allows us to explore this gap, and, if it exists, make it explicit to the person we are working with and help them make conscious decisions about how they would like to live their life. As such, MI aims to help someone to be the best person they can be – to achieve their hopes and values.

Ambivalence and how to understand and work with it runs through the whole of this book. One way of thinking about it is in terms of the things that stop us achieving the life we want to live. Here we want to consider the way people often respond when we talk to them about an issue that they are ambivalent about. In MI, these common responses are called 'resistance' and 'change talk'. They are key elements of the theory of change that underlies MI.

WHAT IS 'RESISTANCE' AND WHY IS IT SO IMPORTANT?

The way in which we understand and respond to 'resistance' from the people we work with is a hugely important element of whether we can effectively help people. Here, resistance means any form of non-co-operation. It might be verbal challenge, disagreement or even aggression; it includes behavioural non-cooperation, such as not letting professionals into the home or not attending appointments, or not changing behaviours despite saying they would. If we are to do effective work with children and families, we need to understand what resistance is, what the multiple causes of it might be, and most importantly what we can do to work effectively with it.

The history of helping people, the whole of counselling and therapeutic thinking and practice, can be thought of as founded on the concept of resistance. There is a paradox at the heart of most helping relationships: while the person receiving help may acknowledge that they have an issue, they find it difficult to change. Freud (1923) responded to this conundrum by developing the concept of defence mechanisms and a tripartite version of personality, where id (basic urges), ego (our conscious self) and super-ego (sense of right and wrong developed through socialisation) were in constant struggle. This struggle explained client resistance. Defence mechanisms against change or even recognising problems included many that might be unhelpful, such as repression (pushing unwanted memories or emotions into the unconscious), rationalisation (providing rational explanations when in fact there were other motivations) or reaction formation (acting the opposite way to one's desires, such as dealing with uncomfortable homosexual feelings by taking a homophobic stance). Defence mechanisms might also be more positive – for instance, sublimation (finding an appropriate channel for potentially inappropriate feelings), such as channelling feelings of violence into sport. The point here, however, is not to introduce Freudian theory, but rather to highlight that much of it can be seen as an attempt to understand and work with the fact that we human beings are often rather self-defeating and do not find change easy or straightforward.

Most, perhaps all, forms of counselling have ways of explaining the resistance to change that is a key feature of the helping relationship. This is sometimes explicit. In systemic therapy, for instance, systems (such as a family) are considered to strive for homeostasis – a state of stability – which makes them resistant to change (Bateson 1972). In other forms, it is more implicit. For example, cognitive behavioural therapy (CBT) arose in part in response to the problems people had making behaviour changes. Our negative thoughts – 'I am useless', 'this will never work' – were identified as crucial barriers to behaviour change, and therefore CBT directly seeks to address these barriers (Greimel and Kröner-Herwig 2011). Solution-focused therapy posits that too much focus on problems leads people to be demotivated and unlikely to change; the answer is a focus on solutions and achievable changes (O'Connell 2012). In fact, most – maybe all – therapeutic ways of working have some sort of theory about how or why people resist change or do not find change easy, and what they might do about it. This is unsurprising: therapeutic help is only needed when change is hard, because we make easy changes without help. Therapies therefore need to have some explanation about why change may be difficult and what can be done about it.

An unusual feature of the conceptualisation of resistance in MI – and one of the reasons we think that MI can make a particularly helpful contribution to the field of child protection – is that MI sees resistance as produced to a large degree by what helpers do or do not do: how we behave and talk when we try to help people. This is an important idea, and one with revolutionary potential for informing how we help people. For MI, resistance is not something that exists primarily within the other person – as perhaps posited by Freudian theory, and often assumed by workers. MI sees resistance, at least in part, as a response to the approach we take as helpers. It is produced in interaction. This is not an insight that is unique to MI, but MI provides the most in-depth and evidence-based way of understanding and working with resistance that we know of. What do we mean by resistance being produced through interaction?

One of the key features of the more confrontational approaches that were common in alcohol treatment before MI and other approaches was that they encountered a lot of resistance. When people were told their drinking was a problem, or that they needed to stop, they would often counter this by saying things that minimised or denied the problem. In contrast, when William Miller used the Rogerian listening skills of person-centred counselling, he encountered very little resistance, and he found he could reduce what resistance he experienced by spending time genuinely trying to understand and demonstrate understanding of the person's point of view. This led to a foundational insight for MI: resistance is something we can increase or reduce depending how we talk to people (Miller 1983).

Specifically, when we confront people, they tend to defend their position. In the same way as if we are physically pushed, we are likely to hold our ground, so if our behaviour is challenged – if we are told what we are doing is wrong or we must change – we tend to defend ourselves. In contrast, when someone is not trying to challenge us, but is genuinely trying to understand what is going on for us, then there is far less resistance.

In many respects, this element of MI is akin to Aesop's fable of the sun and the wind. In the fable, the sun and the wind are arguing over which of them is more powerful. They see a man walking along the road and decide that they will settle the argument by seeing which can take off his cloak. The wind goes first, blowing at the man's cloak, tugging and pulling. The cloak swirls in the wind, but the more the wind blows, the more the man holds the cloak tightly. As the storm reaches its peak, the man is holding the cloak tightly to himself, against the full might of the wind. Out of puff, the wind gives up, saying there is no way that the cloak can be taken from the man.

The sun takes her turn. The wind is gone, and the sun starts to shine. The man loosens his grip, and as he starts to warm up, lets the cloak hang loose. You know what happens next: the sun's warm rays make the man so hot that he takes off the cloak. The sun has proved she is more powerful than the wind – and has simultaneously shown that warmth can often achieve what confrontation cannot.

This is a wise story, which surely resonates with all of us. If you think about anything you are having difficulty changing – for instance, a behaviour that you feel you should do less or more of than you do – if someone comes and talks to you in a confrontational manner, then you will almost certainly experience annoyance, perhaps shame and discomfort. Chances are that you will push back. That might be by arguing or justifying why you haven't (or can't) change, or it might be by minimising the problem or denying it exists. If direct confrontation is not for you, or you do not feel you can push back, then perhaps you will simply appear to acquiesce without actually having any intention of changing. In contrast, if someone talks to you in a caring way, genuinely wanting to understand how you feel about something and demonstrating understanding without judging, then the likelihood of you pushing back and resisting is far lower.

This clinical insight has strong research evidence. Research has identified that counsellors can increase or reduce the amount of resistance there is in an interview through the way that they talk to people. Miller, Benefield and Tonigan (2001) found, for instance, that when counsellors adopted a more confrontational manner of speaking, clients were more likely to argue with the therapist or deny problems. Perhaps even more importantly, increased resistance is associated with poor outcomes. In the same study, the authors found that the level of resistance identified in interviews was correlated with poor drinking outcomes one year later. In other words, when interviews created a lot of resistance from people, those people were less likely to change their behaviour. It is therefore essential that helping professionals avoid approaches that are more likely to generate resistance. As we will discuss further below, these relationships are not confined to alcohol misuse; we have found them in child and family social work conversations (Forrester *et al.* 2008b).

THE 'RIGHTING REFLEX' – WHY WE OFTEN ACCIDENTALLY CREATE RESISTANCE

In theory, this sounds relatively straightforward: a compassionate approach is less likely to evoke resistance than a confrontational one. However, confrontation is not always easy to recognise in practice. We often think of confrontation as being aggressive in nature (like the wind in Aesop's fable), yet it can be far more subtle than that. For example, in these two short extracts from a conversation, a social worker and a father are discussing a non-molestation order. The order prohibits the father from contacting the mother. The social worker says very plainly:

You're not allowed to contact Danielle as per the non-molestation order.

The father, a bit later in the discussion, says just as plainly:

I've gone against the order because I want to see my son.

Here, it is easy to see how the father is pushing back against what the social worker wants. They are being directly confrontational, in the sense of explicitly disagreeing.

But confrontation can in fact take many different guises. In MI, one of the ways in which confrontation can be understood is in terms of the 'righting reflex'. The righting reflex is a term used to describe any attempts by the helper to try to 'fix' the problem by correcting, persuading, educating, offering solutions or providing the reasons for change (Miller and Rollnick 2013). Crucially, it usually comes from a good place. Most helping professionals go into their job wanting to make things better for people. So, when people tell us they have a problem, we often rush towards a solution. The difficulty with this is that we often don't realise when we are being confrontational, and get frustrated when people do not respond positively to our well-meaning interventions. In this extract, the conversation is between a social worker and a mother who is having difficulty with her son's behaviour at school. The social worker is friendly, and you can imagine them walking away from the meeting feeling that they had been helpful. We are not saying that this is a poor example of practice, but considered from an MI perspective, the worker is trying to 'fix' the problem, and there are dangers in such an approach:

> **Social worker**: So, this has been going on for just over a week. Did something in particular happen before he started to feel unhappy?
>
> **Mother**: I felt ill; I was uncomfortable with the situation.
>
> **Social worker**: OK, but you know you've got people you can go to if you're feeling uncomfortable.
>
> **Mother**: Yeah, but they can't even do nothing. Like, they don't really understand.
>
> **Social worker**: When you're feeling uncomfortable or about anything?
>
> **Mother**: When I tell them to sort it out, they don't sort it out.
>
> **Social worker**: I think we need to kind of look at it both ways. If I said like a filter, do you know what a filter is?

The social worker here wants the best for the mother and is offering a lot of suggestions. Her manner is kind and caring. Yet she is not really getting anywhere. Her suggestions are being resisted by the mother. This is a type of interaction we see very often. What is going on?

⏸ PAUSE AND CONSIDER…

- Why is the mother 'resisting' the attempts by the social worker to be helpful?

- How can what we have read so far help us understand this?

- What different approach by the social worker might be more effective?

RESISTANCE AND AMBIVALENCE

To understand why increasing resistance may make outcomes worse for people, let's return to the concept of ambivalence. When we are ambivalent, we often have competing and contradictory feelings and thoughts about a problem and what we should do about it. Ironically, when someone uses the righting reflex (even if they are trying to help), it tends to result in us making the arguments for *not* changing. You can see that in the extract above. Indeed, much of resistance can be seen as a person making the arguments to not change. MI theory refers to this as *sustain talk*. It is simply one side of a person's ambivalence. The problem with sustain talk is that people tend to commit to what they hear themselves say out loud. A large part of MI is therefore dedicated to avoiding confrontation as it is likely to result in people making arguments not to change, which makes them less likely to change. Perversely, direct challenge tends to result in people talking themselves out of changing. We are, of course, aware that child protection practice often requires professionals to disagree with parents, not least when it appears that the child is not safe. Indeed, the fact that MI provides both insights and skills for constructive disagreement is one of the reasons it seems such a good fit for child and family social work. We return to these issues in later chapters.

There are other types of resistance that we will consider as we move towards more advanced levels of practice. In current MI theory, the original formulation of resistance is broken down into sustain talk (where the person starts making the arguments for not changing) and discord (where they are not happy with the helping relationship). This distinction reflects a key aspect of MI theory, namely that resistance is not a character trait or something that exists in 'difficult people' but rather something that is created within the interaction. In the context of child protection, resistance can be created by many other factors, including fear, shame and a wish not to have abuse or neglect uncovered. Furthermore, the whole relationship is underpinned by the power afforded to social workers by the state. You might argue that if you were trying to design a system to create resistance within relationships, you would end up with something not too dissimilar to what we have in child and family social work today. Yet effective helping requires the worker to address resistance resulting from any of these potential sources, and this requires a high level of skill.

CHANGE TALK

Change talk is the opposite of sustain talk. Where sustain talk involves minimising the nature of the problem, the impact it may have or the need to take action, change talk involves acknowledging the behaviour as a problem, or indicating that it is something that you want or need to do something about. In this sense, change talk represents a person's possible motivations for change. It is the other side of their ambivalence. Much like sustain talk or resistance, change talk is highly responsive to the approach of the helper.

A key aspect of MI theory is the idea that people tend to commit to what they hear themselves say out loud. Therefore, if a person articulates more of their own reasons for change, and fewer of their own reasons for not changing, this is likely to increase their motivation and readiness to take action. An extensive body of research has explored this idea by looking at the relationship between change talk, sustain talk and outcomes. The findings are complex but, generally speaking, indicate that people who offer more change talk than sustain talk are more likely to make changes (Magill *et al.* 2018). It is for this reason that a key goal in MI is to talk to people in ways that help to elicit change talk and lessen the likelihood of sustain talk or resistance. Before we think about what we need to do to achieve this – reviewing the core skills of MI – we need to be able to identify change talk when we are talking to people.

Miller and Rollnick (2013) developed a memorable acronym for outlining different types of change talk: DARN-CAT. DARN language expresses possible motivations for change, while CAT language expresses something more tangible, moving closer to actual change. This stands for desire, ability, reason, need, commitment, activation and taking steps. In Table 2.2 we provide more detail and an example for each type of change talk, using the illustration of a mother with an alcohol problem who is pregnant.

Table 2.2   Types of change talk: DARN-CAT

Type of change talk	Example
Desire – wanting to change	I'd like to be able to drink a bit less.
Ability – ability to change	I could stop if I really needed to; I've done it in the past.
Reasons – providing reasons to change	The midwife told me about foetal alcohol syndrome. I do worry about it.
Need – reasons so strong they feel they must change	I know I need to cut down. I can't let my baby be taken away from me.

Commitment – stating that they will change	I am going to give up drinking. My baby comes first.
Activation – indicates readiness to take action	I'm willing to go to one session at the alcohol service.
Taking steps – has already taken action	I called the alcohol service about an appointment.

Any expression of change talk signals some level of motivation to change. However, research has found that some types of change talk are more likely to predict outcome than others. Amrhein *et al.* (2003) found that while there was no link between DARN language and actual change, CAT language, and in particular the strength of this language were associated with a positive outcome. Current thinking likens the different types of change talk to a plane about to take off. DARN language is like the plane accelerating along the runway – providing the impetus needed for change but not in itself creating lift off. CAT language can be likened to the plane taking off; this is when the journey to change really begins. In this way, DARN language creates the impetus for change, leading to commitment and action.

Once we understand and can recognise change talk and the different types of resistance, we can begin to use ways of talking that reduce resistance and increase change talk. Understanding these different types of language allows us to tune in to the person's viewpoint and shapes the best response we might make. The rest of this chapter therefore focuses on this core element of MI, while later chapters consider more what we can do to influence change talk and reduce resistance.

CAN YOU SPOT CHANGE TALK?
The main challenge with identifying change talk is that it is often wrapped up with resistance or sustain talk. This is a function of ambivalence: people who feel conflicted about change tend to present this in the way they talk. They do not necessarily make our lives easier by making clear statements about one or the other. Take a couple of examples:

> I just think there's a big fuss about nothing. I pushed [my partner] and everyone's acting as if I punched her. Sure, you shouldn't hit a woman. But she pushed me first.

There is clear resistance here: the whole quote is saturated with it. This man thinks the police and social workers are making a fuss about nothing. He minimises his violence – saying it was just a push, not a punch – and he paints himself as the victim, or at least as just defending himself. What is more difficult to see is whether there is any change talk here.

It would be very easy in a situation such as this to get caught up in the resistance. However, MI encourages us to listen out for opportunities for change. From this perspective, the statement 'Sure, you shouldn't hit a woman' would be of potential importance. This fits into the 'Reason' category of change talk. More importantly, it signals something of his values, or at least his recognition of society's values. A key motivator for change is often a perceived discrepancy between our values and our behaviour. Our ability to identify and then work with this indication of potential motivation is central to effective help with behaviour change. Statements of change talk are like the tiny embers from which we may, using the right kindling and gentle breaths, ignite the fire. The first step is being able to recognise these in order to work with them. Let's consider another example. This is a condensed version of a number of real statements made by a father to a social worker:

> It doesn't affect the kids because I don't use cocaine in front of them. I never have and I never would. I make sure they're in bed or I go out with friends. To be honest, I don't see how it's anybody else's business but my own. Yes, I use cocaine sometimes, on occasion a little more than I should, but it's not like I'm using it every day and I don't see how it's any worse than people downing a bottle of wine on the weekends. She [ex-partner] just likes making trouble for me and you're doing exactly what she wants you to do by coming round here.

As with the previous example, there is lots of resistance – specifically, sustain talk – and minimisation here, and it would be easy to respond by challenging the father:

> Your cocaine use does seem like a problem, not just to your partner but to lots of people.

Or justifying the reason for involvement:

> We have to respond to allegations like this.

Yet it is important to remember two things. First, this is in many ways a typical and understandable response to the involvement of a social worker in the life of the family. Even if this father actually thinks – or a part of him thinks – that his cocaine use *is* a problem, he is very likely to respond in this way. Second, it is also important to consider that the protestations in this quote may be true. Perhaps the parent's drug use is recreational and perhaps his ex-partner has made allegations in order to make life difficult for him. Here we assume that for this interview our interest is not so much in finding out the 'truth' as finding out what there is to work with in the person's perception of their situation. In this quote, there are some statements that we might class as change talk. Let's consider the examples:

> Yes, I use cocaine sometimes, on occasion a little more than I should…

This statement might fit under the change talk category of 'Reason'. It comes as part of a longer argument in which the father defends his drug use, and is easy to miss. But here he is acknowledging two things that are important in terms of our intervention. First, that he does use drugs. Such frankness paves the way for an open conversation about his cocaine use. Second, there is some level of problem recognition in so much as the father acknowledges that sometimes he uses more than he feels he should. There is some indication that his drug use surpasses his own boundaries of what he feels is acceptable and, in this sense, indicates some possible motivation for change.

> I don't use cocaine in front of them. I never have and I never would. I make sure they're in bed or I go out with friends.

If we think about change in this scenario being about protecting the children from the impact of the father's drug use, this statement might fit under the change talk category of 'Taking steps'. It is an interesting example that underlines the complexity of recognising change talk. On the one hand, it is expressed as resistance. The argument is that there is no basis for social work involvement because he doesn't use drugs in front of his children. However, if we look at the same statement through the lens of motivation and values, this father is indicating that he already takes steps to protect his children from his drug use. In doing so he is acknowledging that there is part of him that feels it is important to keep his drug use separate from his home life and role as a parent. Of course, this statement may not be true; perhaps he does use cocaine in front of the children. For now, however, the key point is that he acknowledges this is not something he (and, by implication, any parent) should be doing.

More than that, he is showing insights into the needs of his children and the potential risks they may experience.

There are two points to make on analysing these short extracts. The first is that really, deeply thinking about what people are saying is very, very complicated. For instance, in considering the two extracts above in relation to cocaine use (which together amount to just 40 words), we then spent more than 300 words, over two paragraphs, writing about what the person might have meant. And we could easily have written ten times more, thinking about all sorts of other issues that are implicitly embedded into these or any short statements. For instance, how does gender or power or cultural assumptions about drug problems relate to this short extract? MI and indeed child and family social work require thinking deeply about what people are saying when they talk to you. In fact, the concepts of change talk and resistance are ways of simplifying the complicated process of really trying to understand what people mean when they talk to us about change.

Second, as mentioned above, it is normal for resistance and change talk to be intertwined. They are often present in the same sentence or phrase, and being able to recognise the two sides of the person's ambivalence is the first step towards being able to help them more effectively.

With that in mind, can you recognise sustain talk and change talk? Below there is a longer excerpt. It is edited from a real meeting between a social worker and a parent. When reading it, can you identify the sustain talk and change talk? You might want to mark each in the text, or if you do not want to, make some notes about where each is.

CASE OUTLINE

The family was referred to children's services following a police call-out to an incident between Simon and Cara in the family home. Cara was pregnant at the time with their first child. Cara contacted her mother during an argument with Simon, saying that he was being aggressive, and she was scared. Cara's mother said that she could hear Simon shouting in the background and called the police. Simon admitted that 'things got physical', and Cara said that both of them were to blame. No further action was taken by the police. This conversation with the social worker takes place while the referral is still under assessment.

CONVERSATION EXTRACT

Father (Simon): Me and her, we had an argument and it became physical.

Social worker: What was the argument about?

Father: I can never remember what the argument was about. It's always over something silly. It's my pride mixed with her hormones and it just doesn't work well together. We've done a lot of self-therapy to sort ourselves out. When we've been calm, we've sat down and spoke about how we're going to deal with it rather than let it get to that place again.

Social worker: But you've got to know what makes it get to that place.

Father: We've both got strong characters, that's the main problem. None of us like to be wrong. But I've given to accepting that she's pregnant so I'm going to take a step back. I'm going to calm down. Whenever she gets angry now, she goes straight into the bedroom and I come in here. We spend 5–10 minutes apart and everything is hunky-dory. We've managed to work out a lot of problems since that incident.

Social worker: That's really good, but what we'd like is for you to attend some groups for perpetrators of DV and we'd like you to consider going to have a better understanding of the different types.

Father: I know what accounts for abuse. Things you wouldn't even think of like putting her down, snatching her phone. There's so many forms, mental and physical.

Social worker: That's what you did, though – you snatched her phone.

Father: When we argue, she's got a tendency to call her parents and she exaggerates, so I end up looking like a bad person where it was actually both of us, and I've got a thing about me where I don't like looking bad in front of people. So at the time it did get physical and I snatched her phone, but I haven't done that since.

Social worker: But that could happen again.

Father: It could, but we are moving forwards.

Social worker: But we'd still like you to go on DV awareness training. Having a baby is going to bring stresses and problems; there's all sorts of things that come with having a child. We need to plan ahead.

Father: Is that sat in a group with a bunch of other guys who beat up girls?

Social worker: Well…

Father: Sitting around a table with loads of people just seems like pointless competition to me.

Social worker: I wouldn't know as I haven't been there, but even if it is, you'll have to look at what you're there for and forget about everything else and think about what you're trying to achieve. The baby isn't here yet, but if the baby was here, our actions could have been quite different. It could have been more serious. We're trying to prevent it from happening again. Is that something you'd consider?

Father: I suppose…

Social worker: So, have you got an anger management problem?

Father: Not really. I just get stressed out and things that…explode. Cara gets upset over the smallest thing and it winds me up, but it's down to me to deal with that better. I've never had any domestic violence incident until now. It was a one-off. I can't see it happening again because it's just not me at all. It was so out of character. I'm actually a very calm person. Cara's the one that gets angry over little things. Because of pregnancy, she's more highly strung and she starts arguments. But that was just a one-off incident.

Social worker: So you're blaming everything on Cara being pregnant?

Father: Well, yeah. It was never like this before. It's a bad stage and we're already over it. It's not a big deal.

Social worker: But Cara's still pregnant, and even if she does get angry, you need to be able to control your responses.

Father: Like I said, it was a one-off.

We are going to use this extract to think about change talk and sustain talk, but first what do you think about the nature of the interaction more generally? Consider the following question:

> Do you think the way the social worker is talking to the father is likely to be increasing or reducing his resistance (and how)?

The social worker is talking to the father in a way that is very different from any type of counselling. It is also different to the communication described in most social work textbooks. Yet this type of interchange is something we have found time and again in our research, in which we have recorded hundreds of meetings. It is a very good example of what we would call 'normal practice'.

In Table 2.3, we have highlighted examples of change talk and sustain talk from this extract. In this chapter, we are accepting the comments of Simon at face value. It is, of course, possible that he recognises the social and professional unacceptability of domestic abuse, and that acknowledging this is a strategy to create credibility with the social worker. This is a form of a complicated phenomenon sometimes termed 'disguised compliance', which poses real challenges not just for MI but for work in this area generally. We discuss it in Chapter 7.

Table 2.3   Examples of change talk and sustain talk

Change talk	Sustain talk
We've done a lot of self-therapy to sort ourselves out (taking steps).	When we argue she's got a tendency to call her parents and she exaggerates so I end up looking like a bad person where it was actually both of us.
When we've been calm, we've sat down and spoke about how we're going to deal with it rather than let it get to that place again (taking steps).	
I'm going to take a step back. I'm going to calm down (commitment).	Sitting around a table with loads of people just seems like pointless competition to me.
Whenever she gets angry now, she goes straight into the bedroom and I come in here. We spend 5–10 minutes apart (taking steps).	It was a one-off.
	Cara's the one that gets angry over little things. Because of pregnancy, she's more highly strung and she starts arguments.
We've managed to work out a lot of problems since that incident (ability).	
At the time it did get physical and I snatched her phone, but I haven't done that since (taking steps).	[So you're blaming everything on Cara being pregnant?] Well, yeah. It was never like this before.
I can't see it happening again because it's just not me at all. It was so out of character (reason).	
Cara gets upset over the smallest thing and it winds me up, but it's down to me to deal with that better (reason).	Like I said, it was a one-off.

Leaving that to one side, Simon actually expressed more change talk than sustain talk. His change talk statements indicate that he has already given a lot of thought to his behaviour, recognises his own role in relation to the arguments and has already started taking steps towards change. However, as is often the way, his sustain talk also reveals mixed feelings about the situation. Part of him feels that his partner is making him look bad, that she provokes the arguments and that the situation isn't as bad as the social worker is making it out to be.

Quite often, the statements that we are most drawn to as social workers are those that point towards a person's minimisation of the problem or reasons for not changing (sustain talk). This is understandable; after all, it is part of the job to assess and work with risk. Faced with a situation such as this, we are likely to have valid concerns about Simon's minimisation of the incident. The social worker's responses to Simon in this extract are quite common. Faced with resistance, they challenge his perspective and try to convince him of the need for support by pointing out that a baby is likely to bring additional stresses and that things would have been more serious had the baby been born. In MI terms, the social worker was using the 'righting reflex'. That is, they were attempting to fix the situation by correcting, educating and providing the reasons for change. Indeed, beyond the righting reflex – which is about how we try to help people in ways that are often actually unhelpful – there are factors shaping this conversation. We might call them 'protection prioritisation'. The worker's primary role is to protect the child-to-be and partner. In such circumstances, there are strong imperatives towards being challenging.

As mentioned earlier, the problem with the righting reflex, and protection prioritisation, is that it tends to elicit a fairly predictable but undesirable response. In the example above, we see that the more the social worker argues for why Simon should attend the group, the more he justifies why this isn't needed – it was a one-off, it's his girlfriend who provokes arguments, he already knows about types of abuse, etc. At best, while Simon indicated that he *might* attend the group, his responses suggest that he would be doing so to 'tick the boxes', not because he sees any genuine benefit to himself or his family. If we recall Aesop's fable, Simon is, metaphorically speaking, tightening his cloak against the wind of the social worker's desire to help. This is a fairly clear and typical example of the way in which confrontation tends to evoke resistance.

In responding to Simon's resistance, the social worker has also overlooked important signs that, despite his protestations, there is a part of Simon that may be motivated to change. Imagine the path the conversation could have taken if the social worker had explored and responded to Simon's change talk instead of his sustain talk. In later chapters, we will return to this extract and look at how a different approach from the social worker is likely to have resulted in a different kind of conversation. For now, with our focus on covering the basics of MI, the extract has highlighted important concepts in MI. In particular, the notion of ambivalence, how this manifests in the things people say, and the way in which our responses can shape the direction of conversations for better or worse.

Conclusions

The chapter introduced some core concepts in MI, including:

- ambivalence

- motivation

- resistance – including sustain talk and discord

- the righting reflex

- change talk, including the different types – desire, ability, reasons, need, commitment, action and taking steps (DARN-CAT)

- the complex and intertwined nature of change talk and resistance

- the fact that helpers can increase or reduce resistance and change talk.

In practical terms, the chapter focused on *identifying* these types of response from parents. We also considered how the way we talk to people can influence the likelihood of resistance (sustain talk) or change talk. The next three chapters are devoted to exploring these issues in greater depth.

Chapter 3

Core skills

Chapter overview

This chapter considers the basic skills we need to work effectively with people. They are a bit like the 'tools of the trade' for a helper – and most apply well beyond MI. Helping people might be thought of as like building something: a table, a chair or a chest of drawers. Before getting into more complicated issues, such as how to design a table, we need to understand the tools of the trade – screwdrivers, hammers, saws, etc. – and be able to use them proficiently. This chapter covers some of the most important tools in MI. These are referred to collectively as OARS:

- open questions

- affirmations

- reflections and

- summaries.

This chapter focuses on the first three in some depth. Summaries are introduced and then considered in more depth as part of Chapter 4 on managing the interview.

In social work, we have a tendency to talk about important high-level concepts – such as being empathic or working in partnership – without always spending enough time considering the skills we need to do these things. This chapter focuses on these basic skills, the tools of our trade, while later chapters outline in more detail how we can use them to achieve aims such as 'working in partnership'.

In Chapter 1 we discussed the origins of MI, including its roots in humanist psychology and the work of Carl Rogers. Much – though not all – of MI consists of using the core skills of Rogerian counselling outlined in this chapter to build an effective helping relationship with somebody. At the heart of this is the idea that we not only need to *understand* how someone is feeling and thinking, but also need to be able to *demonstrate* to them that we have understood them. If we are able to do this, we reduce resistance, increase engagement and are more likely to promote change talk. The skills of this chapter are therefore essential for MI, but they have much broader application. They are probably important for effective helping of almost any sort.

Introduction

We start with a note of caution: the skills described here seem simple. Many of us assume that we can use them effortlessly. In fact, our research consistently suggests that child and family social workers use these skills far less than you might expect (Forrester *et al.* 2008b; Lynch *et al.* 2019). This may be in part because they seem so simple that we assume we can already do them – and so we move on to more complicated aspects of good practice. Yet while most people can kick a football, few can thread a pass like Messi, and even fewer can do so when under pressure. It is similar with 'open questions' or 'reflections'. Most of us can think of an open question or a reflection when we have all the time in the world, but fewer find it easy to do when in the middle of a really difficult conversation. Only the most skilled workers can reliably find that really good question or reflection, one that shows a deep understanding of the other person. Having read this chapter, we hope you will have a strong knowledge of what these skills are, but being able to ask the right question, or use a reflection that shows your empathy even when you're under pressure and when the discussion is difficult – well, that is the work of a lifetime!

Questions, questions, questions!

Our research has found that child and family social workers ask a lot of questions. Yet we often have the sense that they rely too much on one particular type of question. Broadly speaking, there are two types of question: open and closed. Each of these has a purpose, and a skilled helper should know when to use which type. It is not that one is right and the other wrong, but rather that one is (metaphorically) a chisel and the other a screwdriver – they may look superficially similar but they serve different purposes – so you should be clear why you are using a particular type of question.

Closed questions

Closed questions are necessary to find out specific bits of information. For instance:

- Did you go to the appointment?
- Are you still in contact with your ex-partner?
- Were you at home last night?

If you are investigating a particular allegation or trying to focus discussion on a specific issue, then you might need to use closed questions, at least to some degree. Consider, for instance, the following extract, in which a social worker is talking with a mother and father about their daughter's mental health problems:

Social worker: OK. I spoke to CAMHS [Child and Adolescent Mental Health Service] and I spoke to Neil, who I think saw you at hospital. Is that right? Do you remember?

Mother: I saw him for the review.

Social worker: It wasn't Neil that saw you on the ward?

Mother: No.

Social worker: But you saw Jo after for the review?

Mother: Yeah.

Social worker: Jo wants to see you one more time and then…

Father: I don't think so, we got a letter about it.

Social worker: This month or next month?

Mother: This month.

Father: I don't know, I just give her the letters.

As demonstrated in this brief example, closed questions tend to involve some key features. First, the person asking the question is controlling the conversation. You are deciding what should be talked about and even how it should be talked about. This is not necessarily bad or wrong; often it is exactly what a social worker should be doing. For instance, this might be appropriate because you are investigating a specific allegation and need a direct answer to a question. For example, 'Were the children in the room when the incident happened?'

Second, because of this, closed questions tend to invite a relatively short response. Often they will be single words, such as yes or no. This may be wholly appropriate if you are trying to investigate a specific issue. However, in choosing which conversational tools to use, you should be aware that closed questions often therefore close down conversations.

While sometimes helpful to us as professionals, closed questions do not invite a person to be an active participant in the conversation. Usually, when we ask closed questions, we do so to gather information or establish facts rather than to seek another person's perspective. In the context of many social work conversations – particularly those in which we need to raise concerns or discuss risk – this is unlikely to be experienced positively by the other person. Think back to the extract in the previous chapter – the discussion between Simon, a father, and a social worker about a police call-out to the family home because of an argument. We can imagine that Simon was feeling defensive, worried and on edge. If he was then asked only closed questions, it is likely that the conversation would quickly start to feel like an interrogation. He might feel as if the social worker was uninterested in what he had to say, or that they have already made up their minds about what happened. In such a scenario, it would be quite likely that Simon would become resistant or disengage from the conversation altogether. A common form of resistance to closed questions is that people become rather passive – providing monosyllabic answers and appearing not interested. In fact, who can blame them? Would you want to be involved in a conversation where the other person was controlling what was talked about, and you felt that they weren't really interested in what you had to say?

Closed questions do not always provoke this type of response. Occasionally, closed questions prompt someone to elaborate naturally. This is often the case when we already have a good relationship with someone. For example, in supervision meetings, we have observed the supervisor asking a closed question – such as 'Have you seen the child recently?' – and then just listening as the worker elaborates for the next ten minutes on when and where they saw the child, how they were behaving, what the child said and how all of this might be interpreted. This is largely a function of the nature of the relationship and the context of the conversation. In social work practice with families, such relationships usually require us to work much harder and are rarely a given. Closed questions should therefore be used sparingly by workers. They have a place, particularly to find out specific pieces of information, but they are likely to close down conversations or provoke resistance from the parent. Whenever you use a closed question, you should be aware of the effect it might have. Often it would be possible to ask an open question instead.

Open questions

In contrast to closed questions, open questions invite participation and allow the responder considerable freedom in how they answer. Open questions therefore help to share control of the conversation more effectively than closed questions. It is nonetheless important to realise that the act of asking an open question also involves the use of power, just as asking closed questions does. By asking a question, open or closed, you are pointing the interview towards a specific focus (or at least trying to). In a closed question that focus is tightly defined, while in an open question the responder has more freedom to answer as they wish. But this should not disguise the fact that simply asking a question is a powerful way of guiding a conversation, and that the power often resides with the person who gets to ask the questions, and less so with the person expected to answer them.

Yet it is also true that open questions encourage the person answering to provide more information – and therefore to answer as they would wish to. For instance:

- How are you feeling?
- What do you think about the child protection plan recommendation?
- How do you think [something] might be affecting your child?

In the following extract, the social worker is talking with a father about arguments in the family home and his daughter's self-harming behaviour.

⏸ PAUSE AND CONSIDER…

- Which of these questions is an open question and which is a closed question?

- What differences are there in the response by the father?

    Social worker: With the self-harming, do you feel you're managing that at the moment?
    Father: Yeah.

Social worker: What's helped?

Father: I've said to her, we'll have to have you put in one of those places, where you're not allowed out and you won't like it there, so it's up to you. So she said she won't do it anymore. It's a silly thing.

Social worker: What do you understand about why people do that?

Father: I think they just let things get on top of them, they worry and that. When I get worried or anything like that, I try and sort it out.

Social worker: What's your way? How do you manage stress or worry?

Father: Funnily enough, I go out and walk. Coz I got so many things around me, people from the social, someone trying to get me into work, she doesn't understand my health, I'd like to go back to work for a little while, I've got this place.

Apart from the worker's opening question, these are all open questions and share the following characteristics. First, they invite the responder to talk at greater length than a closed question would. Of course, this does not mean that the other person *will* talk at great length. Almost any question can be replied to with a shrug or a monosyllabic answer. Yet, on the whole, open questions tend to elicit more talk than closed questions. Indeed, as a rule of thumb, if you ask open questions and get short answers, it indicates that there is likely to be a problem in your relationship. You need to attend to this before you can make any progress – for instance, by naming and exploring the problem.

Second, open questions give the respondent more freedom to shape the direction of the conversation. As such, open questions are an essential part of collaborative practice. They allow us to develop a deeper understanding of how someone may be feeling or thinking. From the perspective of the person being asked, open questions are likely to convey a very different message about the sort of relationship we are trying to establish. Open questions tend to imply that we are genuinely interested and open to different perspectives.

In fact, it is probably simplistic to divide questions into open and closed. It is truer to say that there is a spectrum from very closed questions to very open questions. At one extreme some closed questions are more like a police interrogation, while at the other end some open questions may be very brief and designed simply to help somebody to keep talking.

Let us now look at some questions from real practice recordings. Think about whether they are open, closed or something else, as well as how helpful you think they are likely to be:

- Is the abuse happening more often?
- What do you think the impact has been on [child] now that you're trying to be more consistent with boundaries?
- Describe what I would see if [partner] was being controlling
- How did you feel when you found out about [partner's] sexual offences?
- Do you think you're doing anything differently?
- Why do you think the health visitor might have thought a parenting course would be beneficial?
- Can you tell me what happened at school that day?
- Do you understand why that would be frightening for them?
- Have you thought about how you might manage that differently in future?
- Tell me more about feeling bad and what that means for you.
- Is that something you'd like more help with?
- How much are you drinking each day?
- How have you found the AA meetings so far?
- So are you two in a relationship or not at the minute?

You will probably have noticed that it is not always easy to categorise questions into 'open' or 'closed'. Some of these questions don't fit neatly into either category. For example, 'So are you two in a relationship or not at the minute?' does not lend itself to a yes or no answer but equally doesn't actively invite further elaboration in the same way as an open question such as 'What is happening with your relationship at the minute?'

Just to make things more confusing, some questions might not even be described as questions at all! The example 'Tell me more about feeling bad and what that means for you' helpfully invites the person to elaborate but it is actually an invitation – maybe even an instruction – to talk rather than a question. In fact, whether something is a question or not is not just about whether it includes a question word (how, why, what, etc.). In English, a question is generally characterised by rising intonation at the end, and the rising intonation can change what might otherwise be a statement into a question. For instance, consider the following said without a change in intonation and then with a rising tone at the end:

You do not feel very well at the moment.

This becomes important when we consider reflections later in the chapter. It is possible to change a reflection into a question by simply raising intonation at the end of the statement. And people who are not experienced at using reflections tend to do this often.

As noted already, it is overly simplistic to label closed questions as 'bad' and open questions as 'good'. And yet, it is still sometimes easier to see the benefits of an open question rather than a closed question. For example, if you were talking to someone about their alcohol use as part of a social work assessment, asking 'How would you describe your drinking at the moment?' is likely to elicit a more detailed description and less defensive response than asking 'How much are you drinking each day?' However, this is not always clear-cut. Take the following examples of questions asked by social workers:

- Are you having suicidal thoughts?
- Do you understand why I'm so worried about you?
- What about [child] in all this?
- Why would you want to go back to him after he threatened to kill you?

Although the first two are closed questions, they could be very helpful to the person being spoken to (depending on tone and context). For example, asking a direct question about whether someone is having suicidal thoughts requires a straight answer in order to be able to assess risk. A person who is struggling with their mental health might also find it easier to answer with a simple yes or no than have to elaborate. The third and fourth examples are open questions which should in theory invite further elaboration and help us understand a person's perspective. However, the examples above (again depending on tone and context) could be laden with judgement and less likely to encourage a person to open up.

The examples illustrate that questions are more complex than they can seem at face value and may elicit very different responses. The key point about questions is that they should help us understand somebody else's point of view. Sometimes that is about a narrow description of events, but usually questions are an opportunity for us to explore with somebody their own feelings or emotions. Good questions are therefore a foundation of all good direct practice.

Going beyond questions: showing you understand a person's point of view

Asking questions alone is not enough. If done skilfully, and if we listen carefully to the answers, questions can help us to understand what another person is thinking or feeling. Indeed, questions can do more than this: sensitive and thoughtful questions can help people to understand their own situations better than they would have done without being asked. Most of us will have experienced this at some point in our lives; whether those questions were asked by a thoughtful friend or a skilled counsellor, they had the ability to help us see more deeply what our own motivations and feelings were. In the act of verbalising our responses, we often have an experience of crystallising what were previously inchoate emotions and thoughts into something that we can understand and explain to others.

Questions are less good for showing people that we understand what they are feeling. That does not mean they cannot serve this function. For example, if someone asks us whether we want to talk about something, and that thing has been on our mind for some time, this would indicate a level of understanding on the part of the asker. Conversely, most of us will have experienced people asking questions that jar with us; the question seems to suggest they have not heard or understood what we have said up to now. These examples demonstrate that while questions are a good way of exploring the other person's point of view, they are less helpful for showing that *we* have understood *their* situation. In this section, we explore different ways in which, as helpers, we can try to show that we understand how someone is feeling or thinking.

Reflections

The most basic way of doing this is through the use of reflections. In MI, as in most counselling, reflections are about a specific way of speaking to people. It is important not to get this confused with the process of reflection-on-action or reflection-in-action which is a key element of developing better practice (Schön 1983). Here, we are concerned with reflections as one of the crucial communication tools within MI.

A reflection is essentially a hypothesis about what the other person is thinking or feeling. Crucially, it is a *statement*, not a question. As a hypothesis, it can be expressed briefly or at length, and strongly or tentatively. Knowing what to reflect on and how to frame that reflection is a core skill within MI. Here are some examples of reflections, all of which might be in response to the same issue:

- So, you seem a little unhappy about that.

- You are really fed up.
- You seem sick and tired of people treating you this way.
- People keep having a go at you and you have had enough of it.
- You're getting so angry that you don't feel you can be held responsible for what happens next.

The above are all reflections, but they vary in how confidently they are expressed and the strength of the emotion that is being reflected back. Crucially, they all have in common that they are a statement that conveys what the helper believes the other person may be feeling or thinking.

The core purpose of reflection is to show the other person that you understand their point of view. This on its own is often a powerful therapeutic intervention. In a skilful reflection, we hear back our own thoughts and feelings and this can prompt us to develop new insights about our situation.

Reflections are also important for ethical reasons. In a reflection we make explicit what we believe the other person is thinking or feeling. In doing so, we allow them to challenge or disagree with our opinions. If someone does challenge – for instance, disagreeing with a reflection – that is a good thing, because it demonstrates that we did not fully understand their point of view. This opportunity to challenge is rarely provided when we ask questions. A reflection is a hypothesis and therefore offers the opportunity to develop a genuinely shared understanding of how someone is thinking or feeling.

Finally, a good reflection usually reduces resistance. If someone is annoyed or angry, very quiet or argumentative, reflections that show you understand their point of view or how they are feeling are probably the responses most likely to de-escalate conflict and begin to build a relationship.

It is helpful to think a bit more deeply about why reflections can be so powerful. Fifty years ago, when developing parenting programmes, Gordon (2008, originally published 1962) articulated why reflections may be important. Essentially, there are many reasons why we may not fully understand what somebody else is feeling or thinking. These include the other person not articulating themselves well, us not hearing accurately or us interpreting incorrectly. At every point, there is the opportunity for misunderstanding. A reflection provides a feedback loop and therefore allows us to check the accuracy of our understanding.

In this extract, which is a continuation of the conversation we referred to above in the section on open questions, we can see how the same worker uses a reflection when speaking directly to the daughter, Nancy:

> **Social worker**: Is that something you recognise, Nancy?
>
> **Daughter (Nancy)**: Yeah.
>
> **Social worker**: What does 'yeah' mean?
>
> **Daughter**: Most of the stuff I see, it's what Dad said.
>
> **Social worker**: Tell me a bit about that?
>
> **Daughter**: Well, now I've got an understanding that if he don't have money, he's obviously not going to give it to me, so I don't go off on one as much.
>
> **Social worker**: It's difficult to change overnight, but you've got a bit of understanding that Dad can only give what he's got.

⏸ PAUSE AND CONSIDER…

- Can you spot the reflection?

- How do you think Nancy felt about the reflection, compared with the questions?

- What do you think that would do to her feelings about you and your relationship?

Reflections are powerful conversational tools, but they tend to occur more frequently in therapeutic conversations than in everyday life. When social workers begin using MI, they often find that using reflections feels awkward or unnatural. Reflections are primarily a feature of conversations where we try to achieve deep understanding of the other person. This is relatively rare in everyday life. Most people who come into social work or related professions are relatively good at asking questions, because we ask and answer questions constantly. We have therefore had many years of practice in asking questions. Few, however, are naturally skilled at using reflections. This may help explain the fact that in our research we found very limited use of reflections by social workers, unless they had been trained specifically to use them.

As a general rule, in MI one would expect to see three or four reflections for every question that is asked, although this ratio will vary over the course of an interview. Towards the start there tend to be more questions in order to open up the discussion. As the interview leads to a deeper exploration of issues, we would expect to see reflections dominate. Then, towards the end, a focus on planning and practical steps tends to reduce the proportion of reflections used. In contrast, when we listen to social work interviews, we tend to find a large number of questions and very, very few reflections throughout (Forrester *et al.* 2008b). However, when they are used effectively, it is easy to see how useful they are for helping the other person think and talk about what they are thinking and feeling. Consider this extract, taken from a conversation between a social worker and a mother. The mother's son is living with foster carers, following a difficult period in which his father died and the mother became reliant on alcohol. You can see how the worker keeps the conversation going using mainly a series of reflections. Read the extract and think about what the worker is doing, what responses it is producing and why.

Mother: In the past [talking about her own attendance at contact sessions], I would've been late, an hour, half an hour, every time, with every excuse under the sun about how it wasn't my fault. Say there was an accident. So, if it was something like that, it would be like the girl who cried wolf: I'd say sorry, and no one would believe me. And other times, I'd flap a bit and get flustered about being there.

Social worker: And how is it different now?

Mother: I'm more organised. I check the buses and the train times; I get the same train every week for contact. I leave the house at 7.30 and I'm there on time, I can have a cigarette, and not feel rushed. I plan. I use my diary.

Social worker: You keep a diary of appointments.

Mother: Yeah. I've got that now. I set alarms on my phone all the time. That's all part of my disorganised brain. I couldn't exactly explain why my brain doesn't work like it should, but I'm taking steps now to make up for it.

Social worker: It's hard to articulate, but you've recognised how routines are so important for you and your son.

Mother: Thank god I'm not like that anymore. I can't be that person anymore. Never.

Social worker: You're very committed to sustaining these changes.

Mother: It's not even committing; for me, the changes have been made. It's like a chemical change – it's built in.

Social worker: It's part of you.

Mother: Yeah.

Social worker: You've changed on lots of levels; it's gone to the core of who you are.

This is quite unusual in the interviews we have observed. The worker has been trained in MI and is using reflections at length. It is worth thinking about the way they shape the conversation – what they do and how they make the other person feel. We think more than anything else that they tend to make the other person feel understood, and that is a great basis for working together.

A crucial point to emphasise here is that social work is not counselling. As we discuss in depth in later chapters, the social work interview is more complicated and more difficult than a counselling interview. We would not expect to hear as many reflections as we would in counselling. However, our belief – based on our research findings (Forrester *et al.* 2019) as well as practice experience – is that where social workers use reflections more, they are more likely to build effective helping relationships and help people make changes to their behaviour. We therefore think that as a profession we need to think carefully about how and when we can use reflections more.

A key challenge is beginning to feel more confident and relaxed in using reflections. And the only way to achieve this is to practise! A particularly powerful exercise we often suggest at the end of training is to try to listen to a loved one, such as a partner or a friend. Take time to give them your undivided attention for at least half an hour, preferably longer. Ask them how they are, how their day was, whatever seems appropriate, and then spend the time listening deeply and using reflections whenever you can. If you do this a few times, it is a great way to practise, and in our experience it is usually something the other person really enjoys too (although it is usually better to let them know what you are doing, as sometimes it can seem very different to normal interaction).

DIFFERENT TYPES OF REFLECTION

As you become more comfortable using reflections it will become apparent that there are lots of different types of reflective statements. In general, the most important thing about a reflection is the degree to which it captures the person's feelings or perspective. Consider these two examples. In the first one, the social worker reflects on an emotion that they think the parent is feeling, and in the second, the social worker reflects what they believe to be the parent's perspective on the situation:

EXAMPLE ONE

Mother: I've worked my arse off, and basically because I didn't look for work while I was on the course, they didn't send me a letter or nothing, but they've sanctioned me. They turned round and said you've been sanctioned for not writing the correct thing on the form.

Social worker: How about food for the weekend?

Mother: I'm going to see my dad tomorrow. It's hard to get hold of him; my uncle's in hospital, so my dad is coming down this way. We've got £40 in my purse, so we've got enough for the weekend.

Social worker: I can see straight away that you're very low.

Mother: Everything's come at once: we've got fined from the school, we've got the vet bills for the cat. They tried to charge us £250. I said we don't have that money; he said come and get your cat and take it somewhere else then.

EXAMPLE TWO

Social worker: Why do you think he told you?

Mother: Because he likes her, and they've been friends for years and he knows I won't be happy about it.

Social worker: So, was he hoping you'd do something about it?

Mother: What can I do about it? You know. All I can do is talk to her.

Social worker: And it sounds like that's hard at the moment.

Mother: Yeah, it is hard. She acts like she's the boss – 'I don't need to listen to you.'

Like learning to use any tools, it is important to think about what the tool does. What do the reflections *do* in these interactions? The best way to analyse that is to see what sort of response they elicit. We think they do two things. First, they keep the conversation going. We need to do more than just ask questions – skilful reflections also keep people talking. Second, they show we understand. And that builds relationships.

However, the way a reflection is delivered is also an important aspect to consider. Look at the following statement and then the list of example reflections that might be said in response:

I'm just not sure whether a group like that is for me. I do want support with my mental health, but I hate talking in front of people and I don't want strangers knowing my business.

- It sounds like you're not sure about going to the group.
- You seem to be saying that a group situation isn't for you.
- You're a private person and don't like talking in front of other people.
- A group makes you anxious and you'd like to explore options that don't make you feel as exposed.

Each of these statements goes some way towards capturing the person's perspective. However, while the content is similar, they are delivered with varying degrees of confidence. Starting with 'it sounds like' or 'you seem to be saying' makes the statement more tentative. Although there is no harm in starting a reflection in this way, when used too often, it can begin to sound quite robotic and unnatural. It can also create more distance between the speaker and the listener. Social workers who are new to using reflections sometimes say that they use these types of openers because they worry about 'getting it wrong'. Generally speaking, most people will correct you if you have misunderstood what they have said, and they usually appreciate your efforts to understand as much as whether you got it 'right' or not.

The last two reflections are delivered with more confidence. Skilled reflections such as these tend to prompt further discussion and self-exploration better than those that are delivered more tentatively. However, they differ in one respect. The first is more factual and focuses on the explicit content of what has been said, while the second picks up on the underlying emotion as well as what the person might mean but has not yet made explicit. Although it can feel safer to reflect back concrete information, it is usually reflections that involve some level of interpretation and therefore emotion that better capture a person's experience.

This takes us on to a second crucial dimension of reflections: what to reflect on. The last two reflections provide an example of the difference between a 'simple' and a 'complex' reflection. Simple reflections tend to echo what has just been said. For instance:

Young person: I'm sick of social workers. You're the third one I've had this year.
Social worker: You're fed up with social workers constantly changing.

This is a sort of 'parrot reflection'. In the same way that a parrot can repeat human speech without understanding it, a simple reflection offers back to the person what they have just said without any level of interpretation. There is certainly a place for such reflections. If done occasionally and with sincerity, it can be a way of showing that you are actively listening and help someone keep talking about an issue while minimising the likelihood of creating resistance. Continuing with the same scenario already referred to above in the section on open questions, consider this example:

> **Father**: When they go out, Nancy's boyfriend gets picked on. He's that sort of person: he gets picked on. Now he's having something done about it; I told him to get in touch with the police and this and that.
> **Social worker**: He's getting some harassment.

Yet basic reflections like these should be used with care. Used too often, they can feel insincere. They are also very superficial; they add no depth or analysis to what the person has just said. Simple reflections such as these should be used sparingly. In general, the deeper your reflections, the more likely they are to be helpful – particularly as the conversation continues.

Another type of reflection is a 'complex' reflection. This type of reflection offers a greater level of depth. This usually involves searching for the emotions that underpin what someone is saying. Ask yourself: what might they be feeling? What could be behind their statements? For instance, let's revisit the statement above:

> **Young person**: I'm sick of social workers. You're the third one I've had this year.
> **Social worker**: You don't see the point in building relationships with social workers when they're just going to leave anyway.

Unlike the earlier reflection, rather than simply showing that they recognise the young person's frustration, here the social worker attempts to understand *why* the young person might be frustrated. There might be other reasons too. Perhaps the young person feels let down by the system or fed up with having to go over their personal story time and time again. This might not be the 'right' reflection, but it demonstrates an attempt to make a meaningful guess at what they might be thinking and feeling. Deeper reflections such as these often go further than a simple reflection by helping a person to articulate what they might be struggling to say themselves. Although we might not always get it right first time, when we do manage to capture a person's deeper thoughts and feelings, it often helps establish a better working relationship. We have all had those moments in life when someone just 'gets it' and the sense of connection this brings. Reflections help build such connections.

The different types of reflection might be likened to an iceberg. Simple reflections tend to capture what is easily visible on the surface, whereas complex reflections attempt to capture what is lurking beneath but isn't always obvious. While both have their place in skilled conversations, the latter is often a better way of demonstrating that we have truly understood a person's meaning.

Summary statements

Summary statements are longer reflections that pull together several things that someone has said at different points throughout a conversation. They are a particularly complex and important type of reflection. Summaries usually strive for both emotional depth and an attempt to capture not just what has just been said but what has been said over a period of time in the conversation. They are a particularly helpful tool for capturing important themes throughout a conversation and can convey complexities or contradictions that may not be otherwise apparent to a person.

Let's briefly revisit the conversation between Simon and the social worker in Chapter 2 (where he was minimising a domestic abuse incident). Here is an example of a summary statement that attempts to capture Simon's feelings throughout the conversation:

> You feel like things have really changed since Cara became pregnant and arguments seem to escalate very quickly. You find it difficult when she calls her parents as you feel as if they only get one side of the story and you're made out to be the bad guy. It's important to you that people understand the real you, and you don't feel these arguments reflect who you really are.

The statement above tries to capture some of the complexities of Simon's feelings. A summary allows Simon to reflect on important themes that reoccur in the extract but might otherwise be difficult to capture in a shorter reflection, or as the conversation unfolds. This is not the only summary we could have offered. Perhaps you read the extract and other things stood out to you. There are multiple possibilities for what you might summarise, and they are neither right nor wrong. The most important thing is that they capture the overall 'essence' of what has been said.

Reflections, like all aspects of good communication, are an art, not merely a technique.

As well as demonstrating understanding of complex thoughts and feelings, summary statements are also an excellent way of regaining focus in conversations that have lost direction or have become 'stuck'. They are a key strategic tool for interview management and absolutely crucial in considering how to manage the flow of an interview. As such, we consider them in more detail in the next chapter and Chapters 6 and 7.

Affirmations

Thus far we have focused mainly on how we might elicit a person's point of view and hold a mirror up to how someone is feeling and thinking through questions and reflections. Yet sometimes people feel too bad about themselves, too hopeless or too lacking in confidence for this approach to be sufficient. Simply reflecting back to people that they are feeling low or lacking in confidence is not necessarily helpful, at least not by itself. That is where affirmations can be helpful.

An affirmation is a statement recognising a person's strengths, value, efforts or worth. In making the statement, you are feeding back to the person a genuine sense of something you think is positive about what they have shared with you. Affirmations are an important skill in both MI and social work, particularly when working from a strengths-based perspective (Graybeal 2001). When someone is lacking in hope or confidence, affirmations are a way of identifying a strength in the person that they are unable to see for themselves. As well as helping the person develop a greater sense of self-belief, this is likely to help establish a better working relationship. The very nature of child and family social work means that interventions are often targeted at addressing problems. Understandably, this can generate resistance from families. Affirmations are a way of making interventions more balanced by showing people that we also recognise their strengths. People are more likely to be receptive to our involvement if they feel that they aren't being defined solely by the problems they are experiencing.

Several points need to be made about this. First, the affirmation needs to be genuine. You need to really believe what you say; people identify a note of falseness very quickly.

Second, positives are not always obvious. This is particularly true in the field of child protection when often families present with multiple problems and the focus is on risks and concerns. In such circumstances, we might need to actively search for the positives when they are not always apparent. An exercise that is often used in MI training is to show learners a series of controversial famous faces. These tend to be people who evoke a typically negative response (a few well-known politicians probably spring to mind!). Learners are asked to develop a statement that captures a strength or something valuable about that person. The exercise usually elicits some laughter, but the point is an important one – in child and family social work, as with many other professions, we sometimes have to work with people who behave in ways that we find difficult to comprehend, or even objectionable. In these circumstances, identifying a genuine strength can be easier said than done and requires a bit of practice.

Third, affirmation is different from praise. Although there is often no harm in offering praise – sometimes a 'well done' is exactly what a person needs – affirmation has a different quality. Whereas praise tends to offer *our* judgement on what someone has done, and is generally done from a position of power (we usually praise those we have power over – e.g. children, students, employees), an affirmation tends to pick up something that exists within the person independently of what we think about it. For example, if someone tells us that they haven't been out with friends for the past three weekends because they wanted to avoid the temptation of using cocaine, saying 'You can be really determined when you put your mind to something' is more likely to help promote a person's self-confidence than a statement such as 'It's really good that you did that', which is less tangible and more reflective of our personal opinion than a specific strength. The former is an affirmation, the latter is praise.

Finally, in the field of child protection it can feel particularly difficult to offer affirmations. In the many recordings of practice that we have, it is harder to find examples of affirmations than it is any of the other MI skills.

⓫ PAUSE AND CONSIDER...

- We estimate that workers are ten times more likely to raise a problem than affirm a positive in a conversation with a parent. What do you think this does to relationships between social workers and parents?

- Why do social workers so rarely offer affirmations to parents?

- What do you need to do so that you can offer more affirmations?

Here's one of the rare examples from our practice recordings of an affirmation. In this meeting, the social worker is talking to a father. His son, aged four, has recently come to live with him, having previously lived with his mother. The social worker and the father both have reason to believe that the mother neglected the child and let other adults abuse him:

> **Father**: Of course, I don't know what happened with his mum – what she was doing. I know she had the habit of leaving him at 8 o'clock at night and not coming home until 2am, 3am. She had no money, no electricity; maybe he was looking for Mum, scared.
>
> **Social worker**: And we don't know about the other people in the home and what might have been going on with them, so there are a wealth of things about the dark and the night-time that he might find very frightening.
>
> **Father**: Of course. And we know he has to have the toy – his Minion toy – it helps him feel safe. If we ever can't find him, he cries, really cries, so we don't know what he's been through.
>
> **Social worker**: And your approach has been very caring and warm, and he's more confident now.

It is possible the social worker found it more comfortable to offer this affirmation because she was talking to the father. It would perhaps be more difficult to do so if she had been talking to the child's mother, because of her concerns about neglect and abuse, and the risk of not wanting to collude. It is worth unpicking these issues with some examples.

Finding the positives

The most important step in finding positives is to be open to identifying them. This is not always obvious, and often the person we are talking to does not see the positives themselves, so we need to be particularly good at identifying them. Let's take a problem-saturated comment from the conversation between Simon and the social worker:

> Cara gets upset over the smallest thing and it winds me up, but it's down to me to deal with that better. I've never had any domestic violence incident until now. It was a one-off. I can't see it happening again because it's just not me at all. It was so out of character. I'm actually a very calm person.

> Cara's the one that gets angry over little things. Because of pregnancy, she's more highly strung and she starts arguments. But that was just a one-off incident.

On the face of it, Simon's statement suggests that he is minimising the incident with Cara and blaming her for what happened. What do you think might be the positives of such a comment? Can you identify any? Here are some that we thought of:

- Simon accepts that there was a domestic violence incident (he does not deny it).

- He has been honest enough to talk to you about it, despite possible repercussions.

- He recognises that he needs to try to handle things differently in future.

- The incident was at odds with his values.

An affirmation would take one or more of these positives and express it back to the person as a statement. For instance:

> - You've given a lot of thought to what happened and are already considering what you might do differently in future.
> - You have a strong sense of who you are and don't want to be violent.

Here are some other examples of apparently problem-saturated language. Have a think about how you might offer an affirmation:

> - I don't see what the problem is. The kids were asleep in bed anyway. It's not like we would fight in front of them.
> - It doesn't matter what I try – naughty step, sticker charts, smacking him, shouting. He's just got a temper, like his dad did, and there isn't anything you can do about it.
> - She says I hit her, but I didn't really. She jumped on me and I threw her off. It's not my fault she hurt herself: it takes two people to argue.

We should emphasise that we are not saying that the appropriate response to these comments would always be an affirmation. Indeed, for several of them a reflection or a question might be more appropriate. In fact, there is no 'right' response most of the time, and whether something is a good response can only be interpreted in the context of the whole conversation or maybe even the whole professional relationship. These are simply offered as examples of affirmations in the face of challenges in finding a positive. So, for instance, affirmations might be:

- You're already thinking about how you might protect the children from your arguments.
- You've kept trying to find different ways to discipline him, even when some haven't worked.
- It takes real guts to be so open with me about what happened.

As these examples illustrate, it can often be hard to find a positive among the mountain of troubles we are often discussing with people. Sometimes a helper has to actively search for them. So where might we look for positives in such circumstances? Strengths-based practice and solution-focused practice have led the way in thinking about how we might identify positives in child protection, and it is worth considering some of their methods as they can be simply applied within an MI framework. However, the search for positives and the search for change talk are very similar – the methods are, in effect, the same – so we consider this further in greater depth in the next chapter.

Conclusion

This chapter has considered the basic tools or skills of MI. These are often known by the acronym OARS:

- open questions

- affirmations

- reflections

- summary statements.

We did not present them in this order, because affirmations are a form of reflection, so you need to know how to reflect before learning how to affirm. OARS is a much better acronym than ORAS, although ORAS is probably the order in which to learn the skills.

We have thus far only considered the first three of these in any depth. So perhaps the acronym for this chapter should actually be OAR. This may be particularly apt. Rowing with one oar can lead one to go around in circles. Similarly, simply using open questions, affirmations and reflections without a sense of how and why they are to be used may lead to interviews that lack direction and purpose. The next chapter considers how we can use the basic communication tools, particularly summary statements, to achieve a more purposeful and helpful interview. We also consider summary statements in more depth, including how they can support conversations in which our goal is to help a person.

Yet a word of caution is worth noting. These apparently simple skills are in fact very complex. They require practice and refinement. Like the basics for any advanced-level skill, the expert practitioner continually practises the basics – like the musician doing their scales or the top footballer practising passing. While moving on to think about how to use the skills, do not ever take them for granted. Time spent practising and improving your basic skills is always going to be time well spent.

Chapter 4

Managing the interview

Chapter overview

While the skills of MI are important, interviews also need to be managed strategically. Skills help us work with people in the moment, while strategic management is necessary to ensure the interview as a whole works. In this chapter, the four phases of an MI interview are introduced and illustrated. These are: engagement, focus, evoking and planning. Key ways of managing transitions between the different stages are outlined, and successful and unsuccessful examples of such practice provided.

Introduction

This chapter considers how we can best structure conversations about change. In their purest form, MI conversations progress through a series of phases. Each phase is carefully guided by the practitioner, and the approach is intended to help move the person towards change. This is referred to as the 'method' of MI (Miller and Rollnick 2013). There are times when social work conversations might have a similar flavour, but they are relatively rare, particularly in the context of child protection. However, all professional conversations need to be managed, and MI offers important lessons about how we can best do so.

Although an MI conversation has four broad phases, movement through the interview is not always linear. Often there is a need to revisit earlier stages, and the emphasis on the phases may well vary at different times in a helping relationship, with more focus on engagement in early interviews and more focus on planning and reviewing in later meetings. Nonetheless, it is useful to consider the four stages partly as an 'ideal type' but also because it allows us to think about how we deploy key skills and to consider different types of strategy for helpful dialogues about problems and other difficult topics. The four stages of an MI interview are:

1. engagement

2. focus

3. evoking and

4. planning and agreeing actions.

The four phases (EFEP) are presented in Figure 4.1. The shapes in this diagram reflect a key feature of the phases. Two of the phases – engagement and evoking – tend to open out the conversation. Typically, in these phases our job is to get talk going, and often there is a sense of exploration and lots of listening. The parallelograms therefore open out to indicate this. In contrast, focus and planning require the opposite: identifying key issues and focusing the conversation. The parallelograms for these phases reflect this – they narrow the range of the conversation. This is a necessary part of effective helping conversations: simply listening and letting a conversation ramble is rarely helpful. Good helpers need skills to help people to talk, but they also need to be able to direct a conversation, gently closing down a discussion when necessary. In addition they need the wisdom to be able to choose which is more appropriate at any particular time. These issues are the focus of this chapter. We consider them in relation to each of the stages of the interview.

Figure 4.1   Four stages of an MI interview

Engagement

The engagement phase of MI is about developing a deep understanding of the person's thoughts and feelings. A key part of this involves establishing a helping relationship in which the person being worked with feels respected and safe enough to open up about their difficulties. This is sometimes referred to as the 'therapeutic alliance' – the building of trust in a relationship. This relational component is an essential part of MI, providing the foundation of all subsequent interaction (Miller and Rose 2009).

The therapeutic alliance is a key component of most effective helping interventions (Messer and Wampold 2002). Rogers (1951) observed that the success of therapy was in large part down to the qualities that the helping professional brought to the relationship. In particular, therapists who were empathetic and approached their clients with 'unconditional positive regard' were more likely to achieve positive outcomes. Rogers suggested that the client's experience of 'accurate empathy' was essential to this process. This involves the therapist using reflective statements to demonstrate understanding of the client's internal frame of reference. Rogers suggested that the experience of hearing another person express their innermost thoughts and feelings in this way, without shame or judgement, creates a sense of acceptance that enables people to move forward and develop as human beings.

These ideas have been particularly influential in MI. Although they underpin the entire approach, they are most pronounced during the engagement phase. Engagement is about hearing what the person has to say and sharing your understanding. It is about listening carefully, exploring the person's perspective, striving for deeper understanding of their issues and demonstrating your own developing insight into how they feel and think. It involves trying to understand their ambivalence, or perhaps even outright resistance, to change. If engagement goes well, then it is usually characterised by both breadth and depth. Breadth involves understanding not just the presenting issue but how that fits into the person's life. Usually, this will include how it relates to other problems or strengths. Depth is about a greater understanding of the issue at hand – for instance, what is sustaining a particular behaviour or whether the person has any desire to change.

Listening of this kind is a skilled endeavour and the OAR skills we outlined in Chapter 3 are key tools through which we achieve this level of understanding. Open questions encourage the person being helped to share their point of view and allow the breadth of an individual's experience to be explored. The worker can actively seek to understand the wider context – historical or social. As this unfolds, reflections will increasingly come to the fore, eventually becoming the primary means of communicating. Reflections offer people the opportunity to better understand themselves and their thoughts and feelings on a particular issue. They also keep attention focused on a specific issue, encouraging elaboration and greater depth. While affirmations do not necessarily help us understand the other person, they serve an important function in the engagement process by demonstrating that we recognise the person's capacity for growth. Together, these skills help establish engagement by helping a person feel accepted and understood. The final core skill – which turns OAR into OARS and stops us from rowing in circles – is the summary statement. This is a key element of managing an interview and is therefore a focus of this chapter.

There are no set rules as to how you begin a conversation, but if this is the first time you are meeting someone, it will be important to set the context for your work together. This is always important but especially so in social work conversations. People are likely to be feeling apprehensive about talking to you and unsure what to expect. At the very least, setting the context will require you to outline your role and the reason for your involvement, and to be clear about the limits of confidentiality. You might also find it helpful to acknowledge potential fears and anxieties and to invite the person to ask any questions they might have. Once you have laid the groundwork for the discussion, an important part of the engagement phase will be to invite the person to share their thoughts and feelings on a particular issue and to listen carefully to what they have to say, drawing on the skills outlined above. Take the following extract from a social work interview as an example. In this situation, the mother has recently left a residential rehabilitation facility for people with severe alcohol problems; having previously not engaged well with the social worker, she made contact by phone and asked for a meeting:

Social worker: I was so pleased when you rang me.

Mother: If I can do that, I can do anything.

Social worker: You are making things happen. So, what did you want to talk about? What else is on the list of things for you to do other than [talking to] me?

Mother: I'm facilitating a group on Friday.

Social worker: You are? Where?

Mother: The place around the corner. I'm looking forward to it.

Social worker: And this is something you've worked out with [the organisers]?

Mother: I think they can see I'm pushing myself.

Social worker: They must have confidence in you.

Mother: Let's see.

Social worker: What do you need to do to prepare?

Mother: Nothing really. I know what to say. I know the rules. I've been there. If I see anyone is struggling, they're not leaving until we've talked it through.

Social worker: You sound confident.

Mother: I'm looking forward to it.

Social worker: You mentioned something else to me on the phone – what was it? Something about your health? You were anxious about it, I think.

Mother: Oh, yeah, I needed to go and see my GP. I need a blood test to find out if I'm suitable for a new medication, something to help keep me away from drinking.

Social worker: That was it.

Mother: Actually, I already went this morning. I surprised myself again. I wasn't even thinking about the needle, then I was there, it was less than two minutes. When I got there, there was no one in the room; I went straight in and out. It was not as bad as I imagined.

Social worker: Sometimes it's almost better not having to think.

Mother: Exactly.

Social worker: So, where are we now? You've been to rehab, you feel different, you're thinking about how you can help other people with an alcohol problem, and you've dealt with your blood test. I'd like to ask a bit about Cassie [her daughter] as well. How would you feel about having that kind of conversation?

As you can see, although this worker and mother have spoken before, there has been a large gap in their contact and so the worker is to some degree going back to first principles and doing some engagement work. By using open questions, affirmations, reflections and summaries, they are starting to repair what had been quite a tricky relationship.

It is important to remember that engagement is an iterative and recurring process. Engagement is always in the process of being created; it is never a task that is completed. While a positive first meeting might help a person feel understood and help you gain insight into their situation, things can change, and it is important not to assume that a person's thoughts or feelings on a particular issue will remain the same throughout your work together. We would therefore recommend time spent 'checking in' and listening to a person's perspective each time you meet.

When it goes well, the engagement phase can lead to lots of talking. Yet simply talking like this on its own is likely to be of limited use. A frequent comment from social workers new to MI is that it can feel like 'opening up a can of worms'. When we use the listening skills of MI, suddenly people are talking at length about all their problems, difficulties and issues, and it can be hard to know where to go next. Simply letting people talk is not MI, but it is an essential first stage towards helping people change. In the next section, we will consider the process of focusing which can help regain a sense of direction in the conversation.

PAUSE AND CONSIDER...

Think about the families you are working with at the moment and in particular those with whom you haven't made as much progress as you would have liked. Reflect on the following questions:

- To what extent do you truly understand their perspective, thoughts and feelings about the issues and concerns at hand?

- Have you been able to demonstrate acceptance of them as a person, even if you disagree with their viewpoint or behaviour?

- Does the person feel that you understand their perspective? If asked, what do you think they would say?

- If you are finding engaging them difficult, what do you think is getting in the way? Who might be able to help you overcome these barriers?

Focusing

The second stage of MI is about helping the person identify the issue or small number of issues that they think most important to focus on. Unlike the engagement phase, which is exploratory, focusing involves strategically managing the interview in a way that helps both participants to be clear about what they are trying to achieve. This is where MI begins to diverge from non-directive interventions such as person-centred counselling. In

MI, the helper is actively guiding the person towards a specific change goal and has a particular preferred outcome in mind. It is therefore essential that you are both clear about the issue being addressed. Although this might sound obvious, we found in our research that it is surprisingly common for social work conversations to lack a clear focus, and rare for the focus to be made explicit and shared between parents and workers (Forrester *et al.* 2013; Forrester *et al.* 2019).

Social workers who are new to MI often tell us that they find it challenging to bridge the gap between the person-centred engagement phase and the more goal-orientated stage of focusing. A key skill in managing this transition is the summary statement. It is quite likely that the person has spent time sharing their thoughts and feelings with you. The summary statement is one way to respectfully reduce talking, while demonstrating that you have understood the complexities of what has been said. Whether it is achieved with the first summary statement or after a few attempts, there should come a point when your understanding of the issues is accepted – because you have communicated your understanding. At this point, you are likely to find it easier to transition into a discussion about the focus for the rest of the conversation.

A summary is a complex reflection that captures what someone has been saying across a period of conversation. It is intended to bring together a variety of things that someone has said in a coherent summary. Often we start with a signal that we are doing something a bit different – with a comment such as 'Let me check I've understood you so far' or similar – then provide the summary and then offer an opportunity to check accuracy. For instance, a summary statement made by an alcohol counsellor for a father referred by children's services about his drug use might sound like this:

> OK, let me see if I've understood. You are pretty pissed off at having to come here. You have always made sure that Dana is looked after, and even though you take drugs, you try to be a good parent. She's loved and really well looked after, and if the social worker had not heard about your drug use, they probably would not have asked you to come and talk to me. You also feel you've had counsellors and drug workers in and out of your life for ten years and you can pretty much imagine what we are going to say or do. On the other hand, life is pretty lonely at the moment, and it might be good to have someone to talk to. You are keen to be the best dad you

can be for Dana, and maybe thinking about how to cut down your drug use a bit might help you be a better dad. Does that sound like where you are at the moment?

A few features of this summary illustrate key elements of summaries in general:

- They are often quite complicated – they are generally summarising talk that has lasted a few minutes to an hour. People can say a lot in such times, so summarising it is difficult.

- Accurately summarising such a lot of information is hard. It requires very active listening. Usually, you need to be operating on two levels. You need to be 'in the moment' – listening carefully and responding to what the person says appropriately, because that is what keeps people talking. But you also need to be thinking about what they have said before, how things link up and where the conversation might be going. Combining the operational (what is happening now) and the strategic (where we have come from and where we are going) is something that becomes easier with practice, but initially it is the big challenge of any effective helping, including MI. It is a bit like learning to drive. Once you have mastered changing gears and checking mirrors, it becomes easier to drive while thinking about where to go and how to get there.

- A summary should be fair. It should present examples of sustain talk, as well as change talk. Particularly at the focus stage, a fair summary is more important than a change-orientated one (which we discuss later).

- It is open to challenge and revision. Indeed, it specifically invites it. The idea is to capture what someone has said.

An important point to emphasise is that we need to think about what to put into our summary statements. Here we are presenting them as a way of finding focus. That is because this is often a particularly important issue in social work with children and families, where there can be so much going on. When we use them later in interviews – to move towards action – the focus is on identifying and reflecting back change talk. Thus, summaries can be used for various purposes, the two main ones being to find focus and to move towards action. In essence, they are a respectful way of directing a conversation.

A summary statement usually helps to clarify the issues and shows that you, the listener, have understood the complexities of the situation. Sometimes a summary statement is not accepted as a good synopsis of what someone is thinking or feeling. When that is the case, more listening is required, but you should not think that the summary statement has not served its purpose. Quite the contrary: you have identified that you did not understand key things and the person you're helping now has the opportunity to clarify them for you.

This is an important milestone in any helping interview. It requires you to have understood what the person is going through and their point of view, and to have been able to communicate to them your understanding. This sense of being respectfully understood is at the heart of effective helping. While open questions, reflections and affirmations all have a part to play in achieving this, an accepted summary statement is recognition for both parties of a shared understanding.

Once such an understanding is achieved, the next step is to agree what you are going to talk about. This is essentially the focus of this interview, and perhaps all the work you will do together. To do this, you need to follow the summary statement with a 'focusing question'. Usually, this will allow the person being helped to select the issue or issues they wish to focus on. For instance:

> So, you have talked about lots of difficulties. Which one would you like us to focus on?

Or:

> Out of these issues, which is the one you would like us to talk about today?

In the context of child and family social work, it is not always possible or appropriate to allow the parent or carer to lead the conversation in this way. Perhaps a police referral came in last night that you need to discuss, or there are several tasks identified on a child protection plan that need to be addressed. In such cases, it is both more honest and helpful to discuss the priorities openly, and in some instances for workers to use appropriate authority in deciding what needs to be discussed. We will return to this issue in Chapter 6 when we consider how we might exercise control of the conversation respectfully and carefully, and consider negotiating the agenda in such situations in some depth.

It is worth noting that the stages of engaging and focusing are not always linear. Sometimes it might feel more appropriate to establish the focus at the outset and then move on to exploring the person's perspective on the issue. At other times, conversations might begin spontaneously, and focusing might then be required in order to establish a clear sense of direction. Providing the conversation has paid due attention to both, it does not matter too much which of the two stages comes first. However, it is essential that they both come before the stage of evoking in which we begin to elicit people's motivation for change. We will discuss this next.

⏸ PAUSE AND CONSIDER...

Think of a family you are currently working with, where there are multiple issues that need to be addressed. Reflect on the following questions:

- What things need to change for you to feel confident about the children's safety or wellbeing?

- To what extent do you currently identify a clear focus for each of your conversations? Is this negotiated, or imposed on the person you are working with?

- Is there scope for you to be flexible with any aspect of agenda-setting?

Evoking

Once we are clear about the issue at hand and have a good understanding of the person's thoughts and feelings about it, we are ready to progress to the third stage of MI – evoking. In this stage, our goal is to begin to help the person explore and, we hope, resolve their ambivalence about change. We do this by seeking to elicit and strengthen their intrinsic motivation. This is really the 'bread and butter' of MI and what sets it apart from other approaches.

In Chapter 2, we discussed the idea of ambivalence and how this is characterised by different types of language: change talk and sustain talk. Evocation is all about eliciting change talk. Our goal is to help the ambivalent person articulate and focus on their reasons for, rather than against, change. To do so effectively, three things are necessary:

1. We need to be able to recognise change talk when we hear it.

2. We need to ask the type of questions that are likely to elicit change talk.

3. We need to be able to respond to change talk in a way that helps the person deepen their understanding of their motivations for change.

In the following section, we will revisit the conversation between Simon and the social worker from Chapter 2 and consider each of these in turn. You might want to remind yourself of the excerpt so that you can begin to see how the ideas apply to practice.

RECOGNISING CHANGE TALK

In order to become skilled in evoking, we first need to become skilled at recognising change talk. As discussed in Chapter 2, change talk often occurs alongside and intertwined with sustain talk – indeed, this is almost always the case. This can make it particularly difficult to recognise. As we saw in the conversation between Simon and the social worker, we are frequently drawn towards a person's minimisation of the problem or reasons for not changing, which means that change talk is easily overlooked. In Simon's case, this was problematic for several reasons. First, by responding only to his apparent resistance, the social worker inadvertently caused Simon to adopt a defensive position which led to more sustain talk. Second, it meant that the social worker missed important signs that, despite his protestations, he may also be motivated to change. Finally, it meant that the worker missed a crucial opportunity to help Simon reflect on these motivations in greater depth.

Recognising change talk can be described as both a skill and a mindset. A social worker we trained once described themselves as 'the change talk detective'. This was a playful way of capturing the optimistic mindset that accompanies MI. In practice, this means entering conversations with an assumption that change talk is likely already there and seeing it as our job to try to uncover it.

ELICITING CHANGE TALK

The presence of change talk is often a good indicator that a person is contemplating change and recognising it as an essential first step in the evocation process. However, recognising change talk is only likely to be helpful if we are then able to encourage the person to explore these possible motivations in greater depth.

It is worth returning briefly to the concept of ambivalence and what is meant by motivation to change. Motivation can be thought of as a perceived disjuncture between the life we are leading and the life we would like to be leading: the difference between how we are behaving and how we would like to behave. In Simon's case, we were able to see that although he feels his partner is partly to blame for the violence in their relationship, there is also part of him that accepts he needs to take some responsibility for what happened and feels that the incident doesn't reflect who he is as a person. In order to elicit further change talk, it can be helpful to ask questions that enable the person to explore this discrepancy in greater depth. In MI, these types of questions are referred to as 'evocative questions'. They are simply questions that are more likely to elicit change talk than sustain talk. We will next consider the different types of evocative question and the ways in which they might have helped Simon to reflect further on his own motivations for change.

Before we do this, it is important to emphasise that searching for chances to evoke change talk is not about clever conversational tricks to make people to do what we want them to. Rather, it is about adopting a mindset in which the helper is actively trying to help the person explore a potential gap between the life that is being lived and a life that they would like to live. The process of evoking is undoubtedly a skilled endeavour, and although we delve into specific strategies, it is important not to separate these from the person-centred values that guide the approach. One way of looking at it is that we are trying to help people identify and live their 'best life' – the one they aspire to or wish for.

Evocative questions sometimes focus on the downsides of a particular behaviour. For example, we might have asked Simon:

- What problems has the violence caused in your relationship with Cara?
- Have there been any negative consequences as a result of the incident?
- How do you think the arguments might affect your child in future if they continue?

Questions such as these in the context of a supportive relationship can often lead to reflection on the problems the current behaviour may be causing. Equally, it is possible to focus on the benefits of changing. For instance:

- What benefits might there be if you and Cara managed to resolve arguments without things becoming physical?
- How would life be different if you were able to stop having these types of arguments?
- How might your daughter benefit if you are fighting less once she's born?

There are times when these relatively simple strategies might not have the desired effect. This is particularly common when someone feels stuck. In such circumstances, it may be necessary to be a bit more imaginative in seeking to evoke change talk, and MI outlines some helpful strategies for doing so. One way to help the person explore this gap is by eliciting their goals and values. Quite often, our behaviour is at odds with our goals and values and this creates a sense of internal conflict which can be a powerful source of motivation for change. It can be helpful to ask questions that reconnect the person to who they really want to be. For example, imagine if the social worker asked Simon the following questions:

How would you like your child to describe you as a parent?

Or:

What type of partner do you want to be to Cara?

Another strategy is to ask the so-called 'miracle question'. The miracle question seeks to instil hope and the possibility of change into a conversation by focusing not on the problem or difficulties in changing but on what life would be like if things were different. Typically, the question posed might sound like:

If you woke up tomorrow and conflict wasn't a problem for you and Cara anymore, what would life be like?

The key to the effective use of the miracle question is to then encourage the person to follow up with a detailed account of how life would be different. In doing so, we are eliciting change talk because the person is being invited to imagine a better life after they have changed their behaviour.

Another technique involves querying extremes. This helps the person to reflect on the best-case scenario if they were to change their behaviour, or at the other end of the spectrum, the worst-case scenario if things were to remain the same. For example:

- What's the best thing that might happen if you attended the domestic violence group?
- What's the worst thing that could happen if nothing changes in your relationship?

Finally, we might use scaling questions. For instance, we might ask somebody to rate on a scale of 1–10 how important making a particular change is to them:

> How important is it for you to make sure that you resolve arguments with Cara without things becoming physical?

The answer in itself provides important information about the person's readiness for change, but eliciting change talk requires us to take this a step further by querying why it is not a lower number than the one stated. For example, if the person responds by saying '5 out of 10', you might respond by saying 'Why is it a 5 and not a 3?' In focusing on why the person has not selected a lower number, you are more likely to elicit change talk by inviting them to focus on why it is more (not less) important. By contrast, if we were to query 'Why is it a 5 and not a 7?' we are likely to hear more sustain talk as they explain why it is less important.

Of course, it is possible that they say 1 – not at all important. This is key information, because people who do not think an issue is important at all are very unlikely to change! It can be worth exploring further why they have said something is a 1. However, MI – in common with all other ways of helping people – cannot help people change if they do not want to change. So instead you may need to have a rather different conversation about consequences (see Chapter 7).

As with any of the strategies outlined above, there is no guarantee that we will elicit change talk. But asking questions that help the person explore their reasons for rather than against change can be helpful when ambivalence has left them feeling particularly stuck. In Simon's case, they may have helped consolidate his commitment to change rather than push him towards a position in which he felt it necessary to defend the incident.

RESPONDING TO CHANGE TALK

Asking skilful questions is an important part of MI, but it is only one aspect of evoking change talk. Helping a person explore their motivation for change in a meaningful way requires a level of depth to the conversation that is unlikely to be achieved through questioning alone. Another important aspect of evocation therefore involves strengthening any change talk that we hear.

Once we feel confident in recognising and eliciting change talk, our goal is to help the person stay focused on discussing their reasons for change. We do this by selectively responding to and reinforcing change talk. Any of the OARS skills can be used to do this, but reflections are a particularly helpful way of enabling a person to connect with and hear aloud their innermost thoughts and feelings. When someone is feeling ambivalent about change, hearing their motivations in this way can be a powerful reminder of why they might want to change. Reflections also tend to encourage people to elaborate further, which is exactly what you want when trying to strengthen change talk.

⓫ PAUSE AND CONSIDER...

Revisit the examples of change talk offered by Simon in Chapter 2. See if you can develop an open question, affirmation or reflection that would help keep the conversation focused on change talk.

There is no right response, but here are some examples of OARS skills that the social worker might have used to help reinforce Simon's change talk and encourage further elaboration:

Table 4.1   Change talk and OARS

Change talk	OARS skills to strengthen change talk
We've done a lot of self-therapy to sort ourselves out.	You've already been making efforts to do things differently (affirmation).
I'm going to take a step back. I'm going to calm down.	Next time you'll walk away (reflection).
Whenever she gets angry now, she goes straight into the bedroom and I come in here. We spend 5–10 minutes apart.	You've already been faced with a similar situation and managed to do things differently (affirmation).
We've managed to work out a lot of problems since that incident.	You've both learnt a lot from what happened (reflection).
I don't like looking bad in front of people.	How would you like people to view you? (Open question)
At the time it did get physical and I snatched her phone, but I haven't done that since.	What stopped you from doing the same thing again? (Open question)

Change talk	OARS skills to strengthen change talk
I can't see it happening again because it's just not me at all. It was so out of character.	You didn't like the person you were on that day (reflection).
Cara gets upset over the smallest thing and it winds me up, but it's down to me to deal with that better.	You're ready to change the way you respond to conflict (reflection)

Ultimately, evocation is all about helping the person talk themselves into change, by recognising the difference between how they want to behave and how they are behaving. Asking the right questions, recognising change talk and exploring this in more depth are all intended to help the person think less about the things that have got in the way of change, and more about their possible reasons for wanting to change. If we imagine change talk and sustain talk as being two diverging paths in a wood, it is likely that the path of sustain talk is well trodden by the ambivalent person. They know it well, are familiar with the sights and are unlikely to need any help re-walking the trail. After all, there are likely to be very good reasons why they have been unable to change. The change talk path, on the other hand, is usually less well travelled. The ambivalent person knows it is there and passes it regularly on their walks, but so far they have revisited the path that offers the most familiarity. We might see our role in MI as a guide who helps the person explore a different path. We can't force a person to choose what path to take, but we can invite them to explore a different route, perhaps one that ends up offering more intriguing views than the first.

Sometimes in social work, we find ourselves re-walking the path of sustain talk along with our clients. There are several reasons for this. First, an important part of social work is understanding the nature of the problem – where it has come from and why it is being sustained. This in itself isn't problematic. In fact, it is an essential part of the engagement process in MI as well as social work. The problem is when conversations become stuck here. The second reason, which is closely related to the first, is that sustain talk often provides important clues about risk. As social workers, recognising and responding to risk is an essential part of our role. However, if practice becomes too problem-saturated, we run the risk of focusing only on deficits and missing possible opportunities for change. Finally, when faced with a person who seems unwilling or unable to change, it is incredibly difficult to avoid making the arguments for change, trying to persuade the person by, for instance, providing the reasons for change. This is particularly so when the possible consequences of not changing can be so far-reaching. However, MI reminds us of what tends to happen when we respond to sustain talk with the righting reflex – resistance is almost always inevitable.

Evocation is a skill that takes practice but offers a way of helping a person move towards change based on their own intrinsic motivations.

⏸ PAUSE AND CONSIDER...

Think of a case you are working with where the person needs to make a change to their behaviour but hasn't done so yet. Reflect on the following questions:

- How well do you understand their motivations for change? Have you explored these in your conversations together?

- Can you think of anything the person has said to you in the course of your work together that indicated they *might* be thinking about change?

- If not, can you *imagine* any reasons why they might want to make this change (even if they have not articulated them to you)?

- How might you use the strategies outlined above to build on this in future conversations?

Planning

If all has gone well by now, we will have engaged in a helping relationship, found a focus for work together and helped the person explore their motivations for changing. If we have been successful, we should be hearing more change talk – a sign that they are more motivated to change and ready to transition into planning. The final stage of the motivational interview is to help the person translate these words into actions. Indeed, it is worth considering the fact that this is probably the final stage of most social work interviews. The question is how we can skilfully and respectfully move towards action in a way that maximises the chances of genuine behaviour change.

The first stage of planning is to bring some focus into the conversation. The person may have talked at some length about their motivations for change. However, if we simply keep listening and encouraging elaboration, there is a danger that we will continue to go around in circles. As with focusing, the summary statement can be used as a way of transitioning between stages and on to planning. At this point, the summary statement attempts to capture all the change talk that has been offered during the evoking stage. It can be particularly powerful for the person to hear this back and an important way of consolidating commitment.

The purpose of this summary statement is to move the conversation on, and therefore we usually follow it up by asking what is known in MI as the 'key question'. The key question is very simple and very important, and it is usually some version of the following:

What would you like to do next?

This question is important for two reasons. The first is that it emphasises that it is up to the individual what changes they wish to make. This element of autonomy is a fundamental principle of MI. The second is that it bridges talk into action. The question only has power after an effective summary statement, and that in turn is only likely to be effective in the context of a good helping conversation. For instance, if we consider the conversation between Simon and the social worker, it might sound like this:

It sounds like you've done a lot of thinking about what happened and are keen to make sure that it doesn't happen again. You were upset that Cara called her parents because you feel like they might have misunderstood who you really are. You've been working really hard to do things differently and recognise that you need to change the way you react when Cara gets upset. Does that sound right?

If Simon agrees, then this is a great time for the key question:

If that is how you feel, what would you like to do about it?

If the person seems open to change, the next step is to develop a plan. In the evocation stage, we helped the person think about the 'why' of change. Planning is where we help the person think about the 'how' of change by supporting them to come up with their own solutions.

It can be very tempting at this point to put on our problem-solver hat and offer up a solution. As social workers, we often feel in our element when drawing up a plan. We might have ideas about local services that could be helpful or know of things that other people have found useful in the past. Providing solutions can make *us* feel good, but there are often downsides. First, a fundamental principle in MI is autonomy: the idea that people are far more likely to make changes when they feel in control of their choices. By prescribing the solution, we run the risk of making people feel that they are being told what to do. Second, even if we have some ideas about change, the person we are working with probably has better ones. If a person has struggled to make a change, they will know better than anyone else what is likely to work and what won't. It is therefore important that we listen carefully to the person's ideas and ensure plans are led by what they believe is most likely to be successful. Finally, it is important that we continue to promote a person's sense of confidence and self-belief. By prescribing the plan, we limit the person's ability to identify resources and solutions for themselves. An essential part of MI is therefore ensuring that the planning process remains as collaborative as possible. The next chapter considers how we might offer advice or suggestions in an MI-consistent way.

At times, people's ideas might be at odds with the go-to 'service prescription' in your agency. It is quite likely as a social worker that there are services in your area that 'match' particular problems. In many cases, there might only be one service for adults with alcohol problems, rather than a vast menu of options to choose from. We saw in Simon's case that the social worker had a particular service in mind for men who have been violent towards their partners. This might suit our needs as professionals by providing a quick fix and tangible solution, but it is important that any plans suit the needs of the people we are working with first and foremost. Not all problems are best dealt with by attending a particular service. This might mean being open to ideas about change that you hadn't thought of, or that might be different to what is usually offered in similar circumstances.

Another important element of planning is strengthening confidence. A person might feel motivated to change but less confident in their ability to succeed. Perhaps they have tried to make changes before but have failed. Or perhaps they anticipate problems along the way. In these circumstances, it can be helpful to employ strategies that help evoke confidence. One strategy is to search for exceptions. This would typically involve asking questions such as:

- Has there ever been a time when you managed to approach arguments without resorting to violence?
- On the day you managed to walk away from Cara, how did you achieve that?
- Tell me about a time when you handled an argument in a positive way.

Questions such as these help the person connect with their internal strengths, resources and capabilities. If a lack of confidence is related to problems that the person anticipates along the way, troubleshooting can be another helpful strategy. This involves exploring in detail what might get in the way of change and the person's ideas for how this might be overcome.

The essential thing when planning is to ensure that plans are manageable, realistic and based on the person's own ideas about what is likely to be most successful. In MI, plans are only made when the person is motivated to change and has decided to do so for themselves. For those of you working in statutory child and family social work, this might feel like a rare scenario. While it is hoped that an MI conversation early on in your intervention will help develop a person's readiness for change, the reality for many social workers is that plans need to be drawn up before people are truly ready or motivated to change. Sometimes this is for good reason – to manage risk, for example. At other times, plans are drawn up in accordance with system-led timescales or by people who actually don't know the family all that well. Social workers tell us that this can be as frustrating for them as it is for the families they work with.

Although this is an unmovable reality for many social workers, it doesn't necessarily mean that an MI approach cannot be used. At times, we may need to put plans in place before parents are ready. However, plans are not fixed and can evolve along with our understanding of the family's needs. Even where there is very limited scope to amend a plan, there is usually scope to explore and enhance a person's motivation around particular issues. We will discuss issues such as these further in Chapters 6 and 7.

❿ PAUSE AND CONSIDER...

Whatever your situation, we would suggest reflecting on the following questions before drawing up plans with families:

- Does the person seem motivated to change? If not, have you done all you can (given the contextual constraints you face) to help the person explore their possible motivations for change?

- If the person does seem ready to engage in planning, to what extent is the plan based on their own ideas about what is most likely to be useful?

- To what extent does the person seem confident in their ability to change?

Conclusion

This chapter outlined the four stages of an MI conversation: engaging, focusing, evoking and planning (including how to transition between them). While the stages are most applicable to conversations about change, we considered the ways in which they might apply to social work conversations more broadly. The importance of establishing a helping relationship as a basis for work with families, finding a clear focus for the conversation and developing plans based on people's own ideas about change have been highlighted as key elements of good practice.

Many of the ways in which we manage such interviews are the same as for an MI-style conversation, as outlined in this chapter. However, some of the challenges – such as focusing on the child, managing multiple imperatives and remaining clear about concerns – are more apparent in a conversation about child protection issues. Approaches to applying MI in these types of interview are considered in depth in Chapters 6 and 7. In the next chapter, we consider how to give advice from an MI perspective; in some ways it acts as a bridge between the first four chapters and Chapters 6 and 7, because it introduces how to raise issues and give advice from an MI perspective before we turn to applying some of those principles into the challenging space of child protection work.

Chapter 5

Giving advice

Chapter overview

This chapter considers how to give people advice in a way that is consistent with the core skills and key principles of MI. You will have already seen that MI emphasises avoiding telling people what to do, and that often giving advice is seen as a mistake – and one that is likely to lead to increased resistance. As a result, people frequently incorrectly believe that MI means you cannot or should not give people advice. For many social workers, this seems at odds with our professional role – because sometimes we have to give advice. Yet, while MI does say that advice should be given sparingly and only in particular ways, it recognises advice-giving as an important part of effective helping. In the following sections, we will consider what MI has to say about giving advice – how and when to do it, and, just as importantly, when not to. We do this for two reasons. First, in its own right MI has lessons to teach us about effective advice-giving. Second, thinking about how to give advice prepares the way for elements of the use of MI in child protection that are more directive and where the worker uses their authority more. The directive nature of advice-giving makes it a bridging concept between the ideas of 'pure' MI – the sort of MI we might see in counselling situations – and the application of MI into difficult child protection conversations.

As with the other MI skills discussed in previous chapters – open questions, affirmations, reflections and summaries – it can seem at first glance that the act of giving advice is quite simple. All of us are probably used to giving advice to people in our everyday lives, including partners, friends, children and other loved ones. And not only to people we know. If a stranger asked us for the location of the nearest bus stop, most of us would have no hesitation in advising them which way to go – or suggesting it would be quicker if they walked instead, if we knew where they were heading. From our own research with social workers, observing and listening to them having conversations with parents and children, it is very common to hear examples of advice-giving. As we will see in a moment, when social workers are talking to parents about problems in their lives, it often feels natural to make suggestions and give advice about what the parent might do differently. After all, most of us, when presented with a problem, can think of at least one helpful thing to try. And if so, what is wrong with making that suggestion? An approach predicated entirely on *not giving advice* is unlikely to translate well into social work. Very often, social workers do have expertise worth sharing in relation to parenting, child development, mental health problems, domestic abuse, the law and many other areas (Hall *et al.* 2013). And, of course, many parents will welcome being given advice (Reid and Shapiro 1969). Fortunately for us, MI does not prohibit advice-giving. By the end of this chapter, we aim to ensure you have a good understanding of how to give advice in an MI-adherent way. This then provides a useful foundation for thinking about good authority and what it means in the two chapters that follow.

How do social workers give advice?

Social workers are often quick to provide advice – particularly to parents and especially when there are concerns about their parenting. In the following example, the social worker is talking to an actor playing the part of a mother whose child is subject to a child protection plan. The worker was briefed beforehand to respond as naturally as possible to the scenario and to whatever the mother said to her. The concerns about the child relate primarily to the mother's use of alcohol, and how this has affected her ability to care for her child, including making sure he attends school regularly. Box 5.1 provides a bit more detail.

Box 5.1   Jeanette and Charlie:
Case study summary background

Jeanette is the mother of Charlie, aged five years. They live alone together and Charlie's father is not around.

Charlie came to the attention of children's services one month ago when he was found home alone by the police at 10 p.m., following a call from a neighbour. Jeanette was very drunk. Charlie was placed with the neighbour overnight.

Following the referral about this incident, checks have revealed that (a) there are three previous reports of Jeanette being drunk in charge of Charlie (two from the police and one from the school) over the last three years; (b) the school reports that Charlie is often brought in late, he is often tired, and they feel he is not doing as well as he could do as he is a very bright boy; (c) Jeanette sometimes seems unkempt and perhaps under the influence when picking Charlie up. On the positive side, there seems to be very strong bond between Jeanette and Charlie. While Charlie may not be doing as well as he could at school, he is performing reasonably well academically and is very popular and seems happy.

Charlie was made subject to a child protection plan two weeks ago. Since then, his attendance at school has been much better – he was only half an hour late one morning. Jeanette has cooperated with social workers and agreed to go to an alcohol service. The school has had no concerns about Jeanette seeming drunk.

The scenario is the first time you have met, as you are taking over from the previous worker.

The worker starts by explaining the purpose of the meeting and asks the mother an open question:

Social worker: I've called you in the office today just to obviously talk about how the past week has been. OK, you know we've got the conference coming up, so do you just want to run me through the last week and how Charlie is?

Mother (Jeanette): Charlie's fine.

Social worker: Yeah, and he's been back at school?

Mother: Charlie has been attending school regularly and I don't know why you keep calling me to the office; it's as if I live here now.

Social worker: I think it's important...obviously, part of our work is to work together with all agencies to ensure that Charlie is getting the best that he can. Now, I've spoken with the school and his attendance has gone up, which is really good, so well done.

Mother: Oh, that's good; at least someone is telling the truth.

Social worker: So, there was just one worry that he was half an hour late on Monday. Do you know what happened last Monday?

Mother: It was just because of the traffic, that's all.

Social worker: The traffic; OK, well, maybe you should need to think about just trying to leave a little bit earlier.

Mother: But that was just once.

Social worker: OK, I know, but it's important.

Mother: He attends regularly and on time, only once.

Social worker: Charlie needs some routine and it's important that he gets there on time.

Mother: People have to understand I am on my own: I have to get Charlie ready for school, get everything else ready, and you know I use public transport – I don't drive.

Social worker: What's Charlie like in the morning – is he easy to get up?

Mother: No, he's not: he doesn't like to get up early and it's a job for me to get him up.

Social worker: What time does he usually go to bed?

Mother: Well, when he wants to go to bed – normally you know by about 9 o'clock.

Social worker: OK, well, he's only five, Jeanette, so I think we need to get some bedtimes in place to ensure that he can get up in the morning and get ready for school.

Mother: He does get up; it was just that one day and I'm not having anybody telling me what time I put my son to bed, no.

Social worker: OK, well, obviously he needs some routine and stability, so I think to instil some bedtimes.

Mother: He does have routine and stability. What are you saying? Are you suggesting there is no routine and stability in my house?

Social worker: No, no, I'm not saying that. I'm saying he needs a regular time, not whenever he wants to go to bed – if he knows he needs to be in bed by 8 o'clock.

Mother: Well, then, I make sure he goes by 9 o'clock; 9 o'clock is fine by me.

Social worker: OK, well, we still must remember that Charlie is only five.

Mother: I know that. He's my own kid, isn't he? I know that. It was just once that he was late; I don't see why people should make a big deal out of it.

Thinking about the advice given by the worker in this extract, we can summarise it as follows:

- It is important for children to have stability and routine.

- It is important for children to attend school regularly.

- If you leave for school earlier, you are more likely to arrive on time.

- If children go to bed earlier, it can be easier to get them up in the morning.

What do you think about this advice? To us, it seems both reasonable and true. Leaving home earlier can help ensure you are not late for things. Putting young children to bed at a reasonable time can help ensure they have enough sleep. Children do need stability and routine. And education is obviously important. So, it is not the nature of the advice that is necessarily problematic in this example. Consider how the mother responds. Given what we have already discussed about resistance in previous chapters, it is not hard to identify points during the conversation at which the mother demonstrates her resistance to what the worker is saying. And as a result, it seems unlikely that the mother would change her behaviour as a result of the social worker's advice. In which case, why might the worker be giving advice in the first place?

We do not think it is whether the advice is 'right' that is a problem in this example, or in many of the other real interviews we have observed between parents and social workers. There are two important questions here – the *why* and *how* that underlie most good practice. First, why is advice being given? What purpose is being achieved by offering it? Would it have been better not to give any advice at all? And second, when you feel you must give advice, how can this be done so as to minimise the likelihood of resistance and increase the chances that your advice will be well received?

When should we *not* give advice?

Whenever your approach creates resistance in any conversation, the MI-adherent thing to do is to stop and try something else. If you give advice and this creates resistance, you should stop and think again. For instance, the worker in this example could have asked open questions about things the mother has already tried (at least then her advice might have been in relation to things the mother had not already thought of). Or they might have asked about the mother's views on education, and how important she thinks it is for children to attend school regularly and to be on time. They may also have used affirmations more effectively as way of highlighting that the mother is already getting the child into school on time for the majority of days (remember, affirmations are not the same as praise). In addition the worker could have used reflections to develop and demonstrate empathy. For example, when the mother says 'He doesn't like to get up early and it's a job for me to get him up', they might have responded by saying 'Charlie is not easy in the morning but you're trying your best because you know it's important to get him into school on time.' All of these things would have been more MI-adherent than giving advice – and we think they would have made for a more constructive conversation.

If there are other ways of exploring the problem, without giving advice, then those ways should be tried first. This will likely reduce resistance and help avoid you giving advice that the other person has already thought of or knows about. For example, if the worker had asked what things the mother has already tried, the mother may well have spoken about bedtime routines or about leaving earlier in the mornings. This would have alerted the worker either to the redundancy of her advice – if the mother already knows, there is little point in telling her again – or helped ensure that any advice she did provide was more tailored to the mother's own expertise and previous experience.

When should we give advice?

The short answer is: only when it is really needed. Certainly, if we are asked for advice. Sometimes when somebody seems lost or uncertain. Occasionally, when we feel we genuinely know something the other person does not.

⏸ PAUSE AND CONSIDER...

- Looking back at the extract above, did it meet these criteria?

- What other times can you think of when giving advice might be the right thing to do?

It is unlikely that the mother had not thought that leaving earlier might avoid lateness, or that her child might benefit from going to bed earlier.

Giving her advice to this effect is therefore unlikely to be particularly helpful and very likely to annoy her. Each of us is the expert in our own lives, and where we are not doing something 'obviously' likely to help, we usually have our reasons. For instance, we may have tried to get up early to exercise but found we just could not stick to the new routine, or we may have tried a diet that we dropped after a few days. Having someone suggest to us without being asked that we should do either of these things would be likely to antagonise us. Similarly, perhaps the mother in this example has tried getting Charlie to bed earlier but found it often leads to arguments and that actually life is easier for both of them if he goes to bed at 9 p.m. This happens not just when the advice is not useful. More profoundly, it is because the worker is showing that they do not really understand us or our problem, and at a deeper level that they are not interested in how we think and our understanding of the issue. They may even believe, or at least give the impression of believing, that we are incapable of thinking about problems for ourselves (to the extent of not realising that leaving earlier lowers the chances of being late). They have not respected us by taking the time to understand our perspective.

This alone would be sufficient to make premature advice-giving questionable. However, at a deeper level, what are our grounds for giving advice? If a parent comes to us saying 'I need help getting my child to school on time', then they may be open to receiving advice – though even then it is better to start by obtaining a solid understanding of their experiences and perceptions. Yet if we unpack the advice-giving in this excerpt even further, it becomes even more problematic. The bigger issue here is the concern about the mother's alcohol use and the child's previous very poor school attendance record. In this situation, rushing towards a solution is unlikely to be helpful for several reasons. First, there is a danger that in dwelling on one recent failure rather than more general successes, we harm the relationship, undermine the parent and make progress even more difficult. Second, do we believe bedtime routines or morning organisation are really the issues in this situation? As it happens, they were not – on this occasion, the lateness had been caused by heavy drinking the night before. (An advantage of simulated interviews is that we can know the real reasons why things happened in a way that is rarely true when we observe actual practice.) This throws new light on the conversation. Not only is the worker giving advice that is annoying the mother, but in fact the whole conversation misses the core issue. The one late morning was because Jeanette had been drinking the night before.

This is an example of a concept in MI known as the *premature focus trap*. Premature focus is deciding too early in a session what issues you think are important. It can create problems when the client does not agree on the focus that you think is important. However, this behaviour is widespread in social work, and is about more than the identification of problems. Very often social workers spend a fair amount of their time telling people what to do, usually in the form of unsolicited advice or seeking to persuade people to change their behaviour and adhere to a plan. Perhaps we need a new name for it. We might call it the 'telling people what to do trap'.

The 'telling people what to do trap' is created by powerful forces in children's services. There is organisational pressure to make change happen and strong institutional understanding of what the problems or risks are. Drift is anathema in many departments. These pressures serve to push many workers towards thinking they know what the problem is and therefore their key role is to get parents to take action as soon as possible.

This means that avoiding the 'telling people what to do trap' is not just about skills. More importantly, it is a mindset, which starts by questioning our right to give advice. We should always think carefully about our mandate for involvement with families and recognise that parents and other family members are experts in their own lives and about their own families.

This means that the first and most important question to consider is whether we need to give any advice at all, and very often to focus instead on eliciting from the other person the things they have already tried and their own ideas about what might work better in future. The best advice, in other words, is that which is given sparingly. Having said this, there will still be times when advice-giving is potentially helpful or necessary, particularly in the context of statutory child and family social work. We will move on now from the question of whether to give advice or not and consider *how* to give advice when you need to.

Advice-giving in MI

Moyers *et al.* (2016) coined the term 'persuade with permission' to describe the practice of exerting professional influence, including advice-giving, while retaining an emphasis on empathy, collaboration and the promotion of autonomy. This means that the worker can provide information or express their professional opinion, so long as this does not involve overt attempts to change the other person's opinions or their behaviour by means of arguments, confrontations or threats. You can also translate these guidelines into a helpful checklist, to think about before providing advice (Moyers *et al.* 2014):

1. Have you been asked directly for advice or your opinion about what to do?

2. Have you asked for and been given permission to provide advice or share your opinion?

3. Have you ensured that, as well as giving advice or sharing your opinion, you emphasise the other person's autonomy, including by noting their ability to discount, ignore or evaluate your advice?

In practice, this might mean saying things like these in relation to each point:

1. I know this is an issue you're struggling with and that you have asked for my advice. I can tell you some things I know other people in your situation have found helpful; I would be really interested to know whether you think any of them might work for you.

2. We've been talking for a while about how difficult it is to get Charlie to bed at night. Would it be OK if I shared with you some ideas about things that I think might help?

3. If I can summarise at this point, you don't drink every day and you know lots of other people who drink more than you do. You feel unfairly picked upon by the school and feel that they are exaggerating how much you drink. Have I got that about right? [Assuming that the response is 'yes'…] In that case, I think it's really important for me to be clear that the amount of drinking you have told me about is still a lot, and while it is your decision whether you stop drinking, cut down or carry on as before, it is part of my role to be honest with you – and I think that attending a support group, even just to see what it's like, could be a really good first step for you.

Let's look again at the extract above, of the worker talking to a mother about school attendance, and think about where these examples might have fitted in:

REQUESTING PERMISSION TO GIVE ADVICE

Mother (Jeanette): People have to understand I am on my own: I have to get Charlie ready for school, get everything else ready, and you know use the public transport – I don't drive.

Social worker: It sounds like there are some days when it is a real struggle to get Charlie into school on time. I've worked with quite a few parents in a similar situation. Would it be OK if I shared some of the things that they found helpful?

SUMMARISING FIRST AND THEN OFFERING ADVICE

Mother (Jeanette): He does get up; it was just that one day and I'm not having anybody telling me what time I put my son to bed, no.

Social worker: OK, well obviously he needs some routine and stability, so I think to instil some bedtimes.

Mother: He does have routine and stability. What are you saying? Are you suggesting there is no routine and stability in my house?

Social worker: Perhaps if I can try to summarise what we've talked about so far. You do make sure that Charlie has routine and stability, and this is important to you. And, of course, it is your home and your decision as a parent about what time Charlie goes to bed. Does that sound like a fair summary so far?

Mother: I suppose so.

Social worker: OK, great. Having said that, I do know that sometimes morning routines are hard for you, and that's why I'm suggesting Charlie go to bed earlier. It is your decision; you know him best. But I know it's an approach that can work. What do you think would be the benefits if you could get Charlie to bed earlier, even by 30 minutes or so?

Of course, it is very easy for us to think up these responses and edit them into a transcript. It would be harder to think of them during the conversation itself. As discussed in Chapter 2, the 'righting reflex' is often very strong, and the 'telling people what to do trap' may be even stronger for child protection social workers. The principles that we have summarised here – avoiding giving advice unless you really need to, waiting until you are asked for advice, seeking permission to give advice and emphasising autonomy alongside advice-giving – are likely to reduce resistance and increase the chances that your advice is helpful (being well attuned to the particular individual and their situation) and more likely to be listened to.

Elicit–provide–elicit (EPE)

If we now take a step back from the minutiae of this extract and how you might provide advice in specific ways, we can think instead about the overall approach in MI to giving advice. From a strategic standpoint, MI uses the framework of elicit–provide–elicit (Apodaca *et al.* 2016). The logic of this, as we have already started to see, is that it is not professional expertise per se that is problematic. What can be unhelpful, however, is where advice is given without first exploring what the other person already knows, what they have already tried and their own ideas for the future. To do so implies that they lack knowledge and genuine expertise – and that if only they knew what you knew, they would behave differently. (When actually, the reverse is more likely to be true: if only you knew what they knew, you would be the one to behave differently.)

If your starting point is providing information or advice, this further assumes that a lack of knowledge is a useful explanation for the absence of more positive behaviour. If only you knew that cigarettes cause lung cancer, then surely you would stop smoking. If only you had known that taking heroin while pregnant is bad for you and your baby in-utero, then surely you would not have even started taking it. And while we can accept that this might just be true in rare cases, it is better to assume that the other person has expertise, and to ask them what they already know, than it is to risk creating resistance by trying to give them knowledge they may not need.

An MI-adherent approach to advice-giving therefore starts by exploring pre-existing knowledge, and what the other person currently thinks about a particular problem or issue. This explicitly positions the other person as an expert in their own life and implies that they have worthwhile knowledge of their own, knowledge that is likely to be highly relevant to solving the problem. You can use open questions to find out what they know and think, and reflections and summaries to show you have listened and understood. Showing that you have listened and understood is one of the best ways of ensuring a more collaborative feel to the interview, even if you subsequently need to give advice. A further advantage to starting the discussion in this way is that you are quite likely to hear at least some change talk. For example, if you ask someone what they already know about the possible harmful effects of smoking, they may say:

> Well, I like smoking, yeah; I go out with my friends, and we have a drink and we smoke together. It's fun being part of that group, having a reason to pop outside; otherwise, I don't know, maybe you feel left out. And so, when you go outside, of course you end up smoking. I'm not daft. I know that smoking is bad for you, but I'll give up when I'm older, not now.

If you have read through the previous chapters, it should be possible to spot the change talk in this short paragraph, as well as learning more about the reasons why the person smokes and the benefits they feel it has for them.

The next step when following the EPE framework is to provide information or advice and to do so using a neutral style. This means without qualifying your advice with judgement or personal opinion. As we will consider in more detail later in this chapter, it is vitally important that, wherever possible, you avoid creating in the other person a sense of shame. Providing information and advice in a neutral manner does not mean being less than honest about the seriousness of the problem or attempting to 'sugar-coat' your discussion of it. For example, if we were talking to the mother in the first extract above about school attendance, this example shows how information could be provided that *lacks* neutrality:

> Children have to be in school, it's a really important part of basic parenting. I know you're on your own, but really you are not the only single parent and that's not a good excuse. When children miss school, they really suffer. Research shows that even missing a little bit of school has a life-long negative impact, and Charlie has missed way more than just a little bit. Don't you care about his future?

How might the same concerns be expressed more neutrally? Consider this example instead:

> When children miss school, they tend to make slower progress. Charlie's attendance this year is lower than most other children in the school. What do you think about this?

How do you think Jeanette would respond to the first of these examples and how might she respond to the second? We suspect that many parents would respond better to the more neutral approach. Before we move on to the final part of the EPE framework, here is one more example, this time of a social worker giving advice rather than sharing information:

> We've talked about Charlie getting to school and about bedtime routines, and you've said that you are doing your best and Charlie is really difficult in the mornings. We have someone in our team who works with parents on how to manage behaviour, and while this support does not work for everyone, I know lots of parents who have found it useful. I think it could be a big help for you, but it is your decision about what to do next. Would you like to know more?

In this example, the worker summarises the previous discussion, shares information about a service that they have available and gives some advice – while also emphasising the mother's autonomy.

The final part of the EPE framework is to elicit again, but this time in response to the information or advice you have just provided. The aim here is to invite the other person 'back' into the discussion, by asking them what they think about what you have just said. You might ask them to summarise it in their own words, to make sure they have understood what you mean, or simply ask an open question: 'What do you think about that?' It is quite possible, perhaps even likely in the context of social work practice, that they will disagree with you. That is not necessarily a bad thing, although it can be uncomfortable in the moment. In fact, if the other person does disagree, it might (and *only* might) be a sign that they feel comfortable enough with your relationship to share a different point of view. Not every parent involved with child protection services feels that it is OK to say something in contradiction to their social worker. Of course, it would be a misunderstanding of the approach to think that MI is some kind of magic wand, and that by using the EPE approach you will always end up in some kind of agreeable compromise. Not everyone is ready to change or ready to think about change. By being clear and neutral when we share information and give advice, we increase the chance that the other person is able to listen without becoming upset and we can continue the interview in as collaborative a way as possible.

Elicit	Provide	Elicit
• Ask mainly open questions about what the other person already knows or thinks about the problem • Use reflections and summaries to show you have fully understood their point of view	• Agree with the other person wherever possible • Provide any new information or advice • Use clear and neutral language • Avoid conveying personal judgement	• Ask the other person to summarise what you have said • Ask for their perspective on the information or advice you have provided • Emphasise their autonomy and demonstrate empathy • Acknowledge there are multiple perspectives about the problem

Figure 5.1   The EPE model

Having now looked at some specific examples of how you might provide advice, and a more general framework for having discussions that involve advice-giving or information-sharing, we now explore some other key principles to keep in mind.

Prioritise engagement

A key aim in MI work is to foster collaboration with the other person, in order to form an effective helping relationship. Unless someone has specifically sought you out in order to ask your advice, it is really important to prioritise engagement, especially when you do not know each other very well. Indeed, when using MI, we would go as far as to say that you should *never* attempt to give advice or share information without first having tried to understand things from their perspective. This can be particularly difficult in child and family social work, when you may be talking to someone who has a viewpoint you strongly disagree with, and where your priority will be not parental engagement but child safety. We discuss this issue in Chapters 6 and 7. For now, suffice to say that listening to the other person's point of view does not mean you agree with it, or that you cannot provide information and advice later on in the same conversation, using the EPE approach. The key is to avoid any temptation to 'correct' what the other person is saying without first showing that you understand their perspective. People are generally more likely to be receptive to difficult conversations, including advice-giving, if you have spent time trying to understand their point of view first.

Support autonomy

If you give someone advice, do they have to follow it? Or could they choose to do something else? Even if we think about a reasonably extreme example, such as being diagnosed with cancer and given an appointment for chemotherapy, the patient (assuming they are an adult) has a choice. They can attend their chemotherapy appointments and do what their doctor advises. But they can also seek a second opinion or ask about other treatment options. They can, if they so choose, opt for an alternative treatment such as homeopathy, or decide to have no treatment at all. However upsetting these choices might be for the patient's loved ones, it is clear that they *do* have these options available. Any court would be rightly extremely wary of forcing an adult to undergo medical treatment they did not want. And what MI says is that not only do people have the ability to make choices; it is by acknowledging them and expanding the person's sense of choice that we can actually help contribute towards positive behaviour change. In other words, denying that someone has a choice or saying that there is only one *good option* available is unlikely to be true, but also makes it less likely that the person will make positive changes in the end – particularly when they are ambivalent about the problem and especially when, as often happens in child and family social work, they did not ask for your involvement.

From our own experiences of working with social workers and training them to use MI, we know this is often a very difficult point to accept. Social workers are understandably concerned that giving a choice to parents or even just acknowledging that they have choices to make may result in them making poor choices. And this is true. Sometimes parents will make poor choices, just as we all do. The question is whether giving people advice in ways that seek to reduce their autonomy and leave them feeling undermined is a good way to help – and we are saying that it isn't. Some workers are also worried about appearing complicit: what if the parent later says in court that I told them it was OK to keep drinking? The key word here is 'OK'. Supporting autonomy might mean saying 'It is your decision whether to keep drinking or not'. It does not mean saying 'It is OK with me whether you keep drinking or not.' When giving advice, using language that promotes a sense of choice can help qualify what is being said – that you are not telling but advising. This includes emphasising that it is the person's right to discount, ignore or personally evaluate your advice. For example, you might say:

> You have told me about your drinking and that you do not consider it to be a problem, or even any of my business. You feel that the whole world is against you and that the school is telling lies about you. You don't like social workers and think that we only try to trip people up. I know having me here is very hard for you and you don't find much of what I say to be helpful. And I accept, of course, that these are your decisions to make. You can carry on drinking or, I believe, you can get help and stop. It is up to you. My preference is that you think about getting help, because I think the amount you're drinking is harmful for you and for your child. I would like you to stop drinking and think it's important that you do so as soon as possible. Having said that, you do not have to do what I say. What do you think about what I've said so far?

Keep listening for change talk

Finally, it is absolutely imperative that you continue listening out for change talk, even – or especially – while you are having a discussion about problems and potentially giving advice. It is probable that when giving advice, you will hear more sustain talk or resistance in return, compared with when you are simply asking open questions and using reflections. If this becomes very extensive, it is probably a sign that you have moved on to the *provide* part of the discussion, without having spent sufficient time *eliciting*. If so, you can move back to evoking. However, even within quite lengthy examples of sustain talk and resistance, as we have seen in previous chapters, you can still find examples of change talk, if you know what you are looking for and *assuming you keep looking*. When focused on giving advice, it can be all too easy to miss examples of change talk. You should continue to listen out for change talk, even when discussing difficult topics, and be aware that it often comes sandwiched between statements of minimisation or resistance and thus can be very easy to miss.

Conclusion

In this chapter, we have considered how to give advice in an MI-adherent way – and thought about when it might be better to avoid giving advice at all. We hope we have made it clear that MI does not suggest you must not give advice. This is a common misconception. You can use MI *and* give advice. And it is not that you would be giving advice alongside using MI, but that advice-giving is part of good MI, as long as it is done sparingly, with thoughtful consideration and within a framework of EPE. Fundamentally, if we believe that the other person is an expert in their own life, then we will inevitably start by finding out what they know already, because why wouldn't you want to learn from an expert? At the same time, in the context of child and family social work, it is extremely common for the worker to have a different view of the problem from the parent, at least to begin with. Giving information and advice in a neutral way helps to avoid making the other person feel ashamed and helps reduce the amount of resistance encountered in return.

In considering these issues, we also pave the way to consider the role of social workers and how we might use MI in difficult conversations. At the heart of the elicit–provide–elicit model are two simple insights. One is that the person understands their situation better than you do. The second is that it is therefore best to create a dialogue about change – and that advice is best given as a dialogue that involves exchanges of expertise. These principles underlie much of good practice in having difficult child protection conversations, a topic we explore in the next two chapters.

PART TWO

HOW CAN WE USE MOTIVATIONAL INTERVIEWING IN CHILD AND FAMILY WORK?

Chapter 6

Power and motivational interviewing

AUTHORITATIVE SOCIAL WORK AND PURPOSEFUL DIALOGUE

Chapter overiew

So far, we have concentrated on MI as a way of helping people, using a fairly standard MI approach within the specific context of child protection. Thus, for instance, we have recognised that this context makes resistance particularly likely, but our main focus has been on how to reduce resistance and engage people effectively despite the challenges of doing so in such situations. In the previous chapter, we began to explore some slightly trickier issues, such as when and how to give advice, and began to think about how to apply advice-giving in child and family work using the principles and techniques of MI – methods that have been developed in and for counselling. Yet social work is more complex than counselling. One of the principal differences is that usually the agency has an agenda, and the worker has substantial power, with an expectation that they use it appropriately. For instance, there are generally issues of concern that have led to involvement with the family, and sometimes actions that are expected of parents, such as letting the worker in or attending a child protection conference. Sometimes there is the possibility of legal proceedings, and there can be very serious consequences of such proceedings, including a child being removed. These differences are a key part of the work of children's services. In such circumstances, how can we apply the principles and practices of MI?

This chapter and the next one address these questions. This chapter focuses on developing an understanding of authoritative social work that allows us to be directive and clear about our role. Chapter 7 considers the specific challenge of raising concerns. A key concept across both chapters is that we seek to use MI skills to create dialogue between worker and parent.

The chapter starts by considering which MI principles can usefully underpin the more difficult conversations that we have when there are concerns about children. Our overall argument is that guided by these principles and using the skills of MI learnt in earlier chapters, we can seek to make difficult conversations into a form of 'purposeful dialogue'. We see the idea of purposeful dialogue as central to good child and family social work. We then consider power and authority and what 'good authority' in social work involves (Ferguson 2011). The second half of the chapter focuses more on how to have purposeful interviews. This involves understanding how and when we need to be directive and the key points in meetings when this is particularly likely to be necessary.

MI principles

The fundamental principle of MI is that it seeks to respect people and enhance their autonomy. This is obvious for much of MI practice, which involves exploring with people their motivations and values, helping them resolve ambivalence and develop plans to change behaviour. How does this principle apply in child protection? Where there are concerns about a child, our primary aim is to help the child, and our work with the parent is carried out to this end. This can often involve a strong sense that the parent must do certain things, whether that is letting the social worker see the child or attending an alcohol problems service.

There are two points to make here. The first is that it is unethical to treat someone merely as a means to an end (Kant 1998; Plant 2009), and saying people must do something tends to imply this. The word 'merely' is an important one in this sentence. Of course, we treat people as a means to an end all the time – when you buy a coffee and it is made and served by a barista, then you are using them as a way of achieving a goal you want, namely drinking what you hope will be a delicious coffee. However, what is unethical is to treat people merely and solely as a means for achieving your ends. This is to not value them as people in their own right, with their own free will and worth. It is almost the definition of unethical, with most of the worst unethical outrages – from slavery to sexual abuse – involving treating other people as objects rather than inherently worthy of respect as human beings.

There is a danger that in child protection work we may slip into such approaches with parents. The organisational focus is – for good reason – on protecting children. We can often see the harm that parents are doing, and it can be hard not to be very directive to parents who are hurting their children. Most importantly of all, we can and should feel huge sympathy towards children who are experiencing harm, and that can lead us to feel that parents have to change their behaviour. Yet however understandable these multiple pressures, they become problematic if we start to treat a parent as merely a means to an end – as someone we can order or manipulate into a particular way of behaving. In many ways, our engagement with MI has been to explore other ways of carrying out the complicated task of child protection – ways that allow us to focus on the child while treating the parent with respect and being clear with them about the potential consequences of their actions or inactions.

The second key point is that treating parents as a means to an end is unlikely to work. It is possible to create superficial change through sanctions such as the threat of a child being removed. Yet such changes are unlikely to endure. Real change needs to be owned by the person changing. There is therefore a danger that if we succeed in 'making' a person change, we will in fact run the risk of the child suffering harm in the future because the change is unlikely to be lasting. Thus, inappropriate or unskilled use of power may well make things worse for children in the long term.

On the other hand, authority is an essential tool for supporting real change when used skilfully. Many of the families where there are the most serious concerns would not change without an awareness of the grave consequences that might follow if they do not. The challenge, and the focus of this and the next chapter, is how authority can be used in a way that is clear and appropriate, but respectful and likely to maximise the possibility of real change. We feel a helpful way of conceptualising this is that we are seeking a form of 'purposeful dialogue' with parents and others.

MI and purposeful dialogue

The name 'motivational interviewing' was chosen carefully. The motivational bit is fairly obvious – understanding and working with motivation is at the heart of the approach. The interviewing element was chosen for two main reasons. First, it indicates that this is a communication style that is not counselling. From the onset, it has been used by a variety of professionals – and indeed non-professionals – in a wide range of settings, including GPs, nurses, probation officers and prison warders among others. Second, an interview is a conversation in which one person elicits and the other provides; for instance, in a job or a news interview one side will usually ask questions and the other will answer. Similarly, in MI the helper seeks to get the person being helped to talk about their feelings and thoughts. There is a clear asymmetry in the relationship, albeit an asymmetry that is designed to be helpful.

In contrast, often in social work we strive not for an interview but for a dialogue. There is still an asymmetry – this time of power – but ideally there should be an equality of contribution. The concept of partnership reflects this, and dialogue can be thought of as the communication style at the heart of partnership working. Dialogue involves both sides bringing their views and thoughts, both sides listening, and an exchange, often characterised by negotiation and sometimes by elements of disagreement.

In child protection, there is a particular purpose to such dialogue. We seek to create and put into action a plan to ensure a child is protected and their needs met. As such, we need a form of *purposeful dialogue*. We are sharing concerns, perspectives and understandings in order to build a plan that is put into action to ensure a child is safe – or at least safer.

Our belief, supported by extensive experience in supporting people who use MI in child protection, is that purposeful dialogue can be achieved using the key principles and skills of MI. However, these need to be used in a way that understands and is comfortable with the power and authority that the social worker has. We outline what this means in the next section, which introduces the idea of the 'authoritative social worker'.

Power and authoritative social work

The appropriate use of power is at the heart of the conundrums we have as workers in doing something like child protection. We want to help people, yet we have substantial power over them, and this makes helping (as often conceived) difficult. The power that workers have manifests itself at every level. They make recommendations about whether children should be subject to a child protection plan or a court order, and usually initiate the process that might result in such an outcome. Plans for court, for child protection or even for children in need will usually have fairly substantial expectations for parents – for instance, about school attendance or cooperation with specific services. The plan opens up family life to the involvement of multiple professionals.

In more mundane ways, workers exercise their power in relation to families in smaller day-to-day decisions. Should the worker call the GP to share a concern? Is it OK for them to ask a grandparent to become more involved with a family? At the simplest level, there is an expectation that parents will be in for visits, and on some occasions the plan stipulates that these will be 'unannounced'. These are all examples of the exercise of state power by workers.

Yet power is not just about the decisions workers make outside meetings. It affects the role of the parent and the worker in a child protection conversation, influencing almost every element of the meeting. It is not possible to understand such conversations or suggest ways to do them well without taking power seriously.

Consider the situation of the parent. They are faced with multiple challenges. On the one hand, they may be aware that they are struggling or parenting in ways that ideally they would not wish to. They may want to change, or at least they may feel ambivalent about changing. However, they are also confronted with not just an individual worker but a series of institutions that have great power. They may push back against professional involvement in their family, perhaps because that is a common human reaction or because they do not want their problems – including perhaps their abuses – to be discovered. For both reasons, resistance is a ubiquitous feature of the engagement between workers and parents (Nelsen 1975). This can range from outright hostility or even assault, through to apparent cooperation designed to disguise concerns and remove professional involvement. More relevant to our current discussion, it often informs the interaction between parent and worker in complex and sometimes contradictory ways, with power struggles between parents and workers played out in the details of interviews. Hall and others (Hall *et al.* 2013, Hall and White 2005) have captured the minutiae of some of these interactions, with parents trying to shape the purpose of a meeting or how they are constructed as parents.

Power is at least as important in shaping the social worker's role and their contribution in interviews. Throughout the interchanges of an everyday encounter, workers are exercising power. This can be explicit

('We need to talk about what happened last night') or more subtle (for instance, the act of agreeing an agenda is an exercise of power). Even in not using our power, we are implicated in the power implicit in the relationship. For instance, if as a worker I decide not to impose my agenda but to let the parent guide the discussion, in deciding *not* to use power, the power I had to potentially shape the conversation is implicit. There is a difference here between a worker who, perhaps through inexperience or lack of confidence, does not know how to take control of a conversation and an experienced practitioner who could control a conversation but decides not to. The former is not exercising power and is therefore not a skilled worker. The latter is powerful, although they are choosing to use that power to engage with the parent in a particular way.

Our belief is that parents and others find it helpful when social workers understand and feel comfortable with the power they have. They will obviously find it very unhelpful or even harmful when workers misuse their power. But they also find it unhelpful when workers do not understand their role or how to use the power and authority that go with it. The best social workers understand the power they have and the authority that goes with it, they feel comfortable with it, and they are committed to using it in a way that engages, respects and empowers the other. This is not unique to social workers. Most of us appreciate professionals who feel comfortable in their role, who do not shy away from the power it may involve, but who use that power to engage us in as equal and appropriate a way as possible. Consider what you might want from your GP or a police officer. Indeed, the same phenomenon has been found in parenting, where neither permissive nor authoritarian parenting seems optimal. Rather, the best parents are authoritative – they have power, and they use that power in the child's best interests – for instance, by setting limits when needed. Because they are comfortable in using power, authoritative approaches often require less overt use of power.

In a similar way, social workers need to feel comfortable with the power they possess and committed to using that power to create as equal and fair a relationship as possible in the circumstances. In particular, they recognise that parents and others are the experts in their own lives and their families. The idea of the authoritative social worker has been borrowed from the psychological literature on parenting, to indicate a worker who is neither permissive nor authoritarian, but able to use their power appropriately.

WHAT MIGHT THIS MEAN IN PRACTICE?

A key element of being an authoritative worker is being able to be explicit about the power we possess. This can often be at the beginning of a meeting or a relationship, where being transparent about the workings of power can be enormously helpful. Or it can be something we explicitly address during a meeting if issues of power, judgement or consequences come up.

The following extracts are taken from another simulated interview, where a real worker undertakes an interview with an actor playing a mother. One of the positive features of simulated interviews is that we can see how different workers respond to the same challenges. In this case, the scenario is exactly the same as the one we analysed in some depth in the previous chapter (the case study of Jeanette and Charlie). What is interesting is how differently the worker manages the situation. They do so in a way that is consistent with MI principles, but they are also clear and transparent about power and authority. In doing so, it provides a great example of authoritative social work:

> **Social worker**: OK. Hi, Jeanette. How are you doing today?
>
> **Mother (Jeanette)**: All right.
>
> **Social worker**: OK? I've come today…remember when I saw you last time, we spoke about, me coming back and having a discussion with you prior to the CP conference.
>
> **Mother**: Yeah.
>
> **Social worker**: So I just wanted to come today to kind of talk to you about the changes that have been made and what I'm going to present when we go to the conference, because I know sometimes it can be a bit difficult for families to be in that situation not knowing what the social worker is gonna say. So, I'm going to be very open and honest with you today. Is that OK?
>
> **Mother**: Yeah, that's OK.
>
> **Social worker**: So, I've done some agency checks which means I've contacted the school and contacted the alcohol service and, I've had some good feedback, especially from the school. They told me that Charlie has been attending regularly, which is fantastic, and he's only been late once, but you know sometimes things happen. And I also spoke to, as I said, the alcohol service, and they said you did attend one of the appointments, but you haven't attended subsequent appointments.

Mother: No.

Social worker: So, what I wanted to do is maybe kind of look at the positive things that you've done, and see how we can work on that; also look at the things you're maybe finding a little bit difficult and see what we can do to support you around that too, yeah?

Mother: Yeah.

Social worker: So, let's talk about Charlie and the school attendance. What have you been doing in order to make sure he's about to attend regularly and on time?

⓲ PAUSE AND CONSIDER...

Compare this extract with the same situation as handled very differently in Chapter 5 (p.96). Consider:

- What is the worker doing differently?

- How is Jeanette responding differently?

- In which extract do you think Charlie's safety is being better protected?

This extract covers the first minute or two of an interview, yet it is already possible to see some clear differences from the same situation as handled by a worker in Chapter 5. Many of these differences can be understood through a 'therapeutic lens'; by that we mean that elements of the worker's talk are consistent with strengths-based, solution-focused and MI practice. The worker shows an understanding of the parent's perspective ('it can be a bit difficult for families to be in that situation not knowing what the social worker is gonna say') and they emphasise the positives – such as school attendance. The final question is also designed to start a conversation about the positive changes that have happened, which is very different from the focus of the worker in Chapter 5, who jumped straight into a focus on why Charlie had been late one morning.

Yet there is a lot going on here that you would not find in a therapeutic encounter. The worker is very clear about their power and authority. This is obvious in what they say – for instance, giving feedback from the school and the alcohol service. It is also apparent in the fact that they dominate the conversation. While they check in with the parent, they hold the conversational reins and clearly explain the purpose of the interview as they see it. They spend most of the first 90 seconds of the interview explaining how they see things and what they want to discuss.

They also emphasise the importance of them being 'open and honest' – and then demonstrate their transparency by providing an accurate account of the information that they have. This involves identifying both positives and potential areas of concern, and making it clear that the parent will have an opportunity to talk about these.

Already we can see that this is a different type of conversation. Compare it with the same scenario as considered in Chapter 5 but approached in a very different way. In many ways, the approach we discussed in Chapter 5 was an example of common practice in child protection work – with the parent being told a lot what they should do, a lot of advice-giving and relatively little listening to the parent. The worker justified this by saying they were being 'child-focused', yet it is difficult to think that the child was being helped. The interview had authority without compassion. This approach to the same conversation is very different. The worker is combining power with a compassionate and caring approach.

The current interview also differs from purely therapeutic conversations. There is much clearer consideration of role and use of power. Therapeutic skills are used in the context of the power relationship, ultimately to ensure that the conversation becomes a genuine dialogue. A purely therapeutic conversation might have compassion without authority, or without sufficient authority for child protection work. In this interview, the worker combines authority and compassion in an approach that is purposeful. We describe this as authoritative social work.

It is worth noting that the above transcript is not a perfect piece of social work. There is probably no such thing. It is a real social worker wrestling with a difficult interview and doing a great job. Yet it is possible from the comfort of our armchairs to unpick elements of it and think about what we might do differently. For instance, consider the following:

He's only been late once, but you know sometimes things happen.

Is this appropriate recognition that being late once is perhaps not much of a problem? Or is it tending to collude with Jeanette – almost making her excuses for her? There is no right answer to these questions, because social work is an art not a science. However, it is worth thinking about what we think the social worker might have said instead.

It is not just in setting the scene that the worker shows they can combine authority and compassion to provide authoritative social work. Early on in the conversation, the worker is trying to elicit the mother's motivations for change, and – perhaps to her surprise – the mother identifies the threat of social work involvement. The worker does not try to pretend this is not an issue, but rather again she embraces compassionate authority and is clear about her role and power:

> **Social worker**: So, what do you think's helped to change your mind about it? What do you think's helped to make you realise that, actually, spending a bit more time with Charlie is important?
>
> **Mother**: I think having his name put on a register, I think, was what worried me the most. I think, you know, I've really cut down on my drinking since then; I'm not drinking as much and, you know, I got a bit scared maybe, that they might take him away from me so… So, that's really why I'm trying to sort myself out and I think I've done really well so far.
>
> **Social worker**: Yeah, I think you've done really well as well, and I'm just wondering, it's OK for me to come and say you've done really well – and I think probably it's important I say that because I'm probably the one that will be responsible for relaying to other people whether Charlie stays in your care or not, so I'm aware, kind of, how difficult our relationship can be – but I'm just wondering about other people, who are important to you, who also noticed the change in you. Has there been anyone who has been able to say to you 'well done', 'you've done really well'?

Again, the worker does not try to pretend they do not have power. They embrace it. Indeed, perhaps in the flow of conversation they claim rather too much power – '[I] will be responsible for relaying to other people whether Charlie stays in your care or not' may not take account of the checks and balances involved in social services decision-making. However, it is a much more helpful response than:

- ignoring the concerns of the parent about your power

- pretending you do not have that power (e.g. 'It will be up to my manager and the court').

Again, the worker acknowledges their power, provides some feedback and steers the conversation to look at positives. The skilled worker is comfortable with their role and the power involved in every element of the work, but they use that power to engage and empower others. In doing so, they create dialogue, a concept we discuss further in the next chapter. This is the heart of authoritative social work.

Having considered what is involved in authoritative social work, we now turn to consider purposefulness in more detail. A surprising finding for us across a range of studies observing practice was that in a significant minority of interviews it was not clear what the purpose of the meeting was. Perhaps there is a lack of attention to ensuring purposeful interviews – ones that have a focus and manage to address that focus – in social work. In the next section, we consider how workers can understand and use directiveness as a way of ensuring that interviews are purposeful.

Purposeful practice

This section considers in some depth key points where a more directive approach in an interview can help ensure that the meeting is purposeful – for both worker and others. Being able to guide the interview in such a way is necessary to achieve purposeful dialogue.

The spectrum of directiveness

In a particularly important contribution to our understanding of helpful communication in behaviour change, Rollnick and colleagues (2005) introduce the idea of a spectrum of directiveness. At one end is telling people what to do: 'you must give up drinking'. They call this *leading*. It tends not to be very effective in creating behaviour change and is likely to create resistance, for reasons we have already considered. At the other end is simply listening. Rollnick *et al.* characterise this as *following*. In the middle is a more complicated position that they call *guiding*. In this situation, we are working collaboratively with the person, yet we retain specific expertise. Like a guide to a city we know well, we may ask the tourist we are working with what they would like to do; we may then offer some options and allow them considerable freedom to explore for themselves, while always being there to provide information or advice should it be requested.

Rollnick's argument is not only that leading has a tendency to be counterproductive but that, perhaps surprisingly, just following often achieves relatively little. We found this ourselves when studying social worker skills. Empathy and collaboration on their own had little impact on outcomes for families: something else was needed. Rollnick calls this something else *guiding*. He and his co-authors characterise this in an MI-like way, identifying how a skilled MI helper elicits motivation, listens, finds focus and helps the person to make a plan. And guiding is not just a description of MI; it is a feature of most effective helping methods. Whether using MI, systemic or person-centred approaches, effective social workers tend to guide rather more than they lead or follow.

Yet a key insight is that effective helpers have to be able to move between all three modes, or along the spectrum of directiveness, because there are times when each is the right thing to do. Rollnick's argument is that we should seek to spend most of our time in 'guiding' mode, but sometimes following or leading is necessary. This is obviously the case for following. Sometimes people just need to talk, and the effective helper may just need to listen. When would leading be appropriate? Up to now, we have focused on the potential dangers of telling people what to do, and in particular emphasised its potential to create resistance. Yet for an interview to be purposeful – for it to allow a shared sense of how and why the conversation is happening and what you are trying to achieve – workers need to be able to be directive. By that we mean directive in a respectful way that focuses on creating dialogue – but directive, nonetheless. One way of thinking about this is by considering key points for directiveness in the interview and how we might manage them in an MI-consistent way.

KEY POINTS FOR DIRECTIVENESS IN THE INTERVIEW

There are three points in a social work interview when it is particularly likely that a more directive style of communication will be necessary. In each instance, directiveness is needed in order to *create dialogue*. These are loosely at the beginning, middle and end of the interview:

- in setting an agenda for the interview
- in identifying focus for discussion and
- when agreeing next steps at the end or the middle.

We began to consider directiveness as part of managing the interview more generally in an MI style in Chapter 4, before thinking about the spectrum of directiveness in this chapter. Here we want to consider the higher level of directiveness that is often necessary in child protection, and how we might carry that out using MI principles and skills.

Agenda-setting does feature in MI, and was mentioned in Chapter 4, but as a relatively minor element of the work. This is perhaps because it is assumed there is some shared understanding about what is to be discussed or the nature of roles, at least in many helping situations. In child protection work and most of statutory social work, it is often more important to set the agenda, as it provides a structure for dialogue and sets the parameters within which the interview should move; and because such work often involves working with a wide variety of issues. Much of this chapter is therefore directly or indirectly about negotiating the agenda.

Before setting the agenda – indeed, before meeting a family – it is necessary to have a clear sense of the purpose of the interview. What is the point of this discussion? This can sometimes be as simple as 'getting to know the family a bit better', but typically it is much more complicated. For instance, your agenda as you think about it while you head up the path towards the front door might be:

> I need to let the parents know what I say in my child protection report, to find out what they think about the teacher telling me they were worried about Ezra's attendance and to find out how they feel after the leak in the living-room roof at the weekend. Oh, and not to forget to let them know we have changed the time of the child protection conference from 2 to 11. And I need to talk to Ezra alone and see how he is doing.

Now, this is quite a lot of stuff to get through – and there are some things here that the social worker *must* ensure are discussed or they would not be doing the job. But here's the thing: the worker is not the only one with an agenda. The parents might see the social worker coming up the path and think:

> Oh no! I forgot she was coming! We really need to show the worker we have got our act together as parents – so must make sure we keep her out of the bathroom because it is a mess. Also, since the living room flooded, we haven't been able to get anything sorted – the flat has been in chaos. I wonder if social services could help with that? Oh no! They're probably going to ask why Ezra has not been to school. But it's hard when the house is in a mess. And then there's that meeting she keeps going on about. Let's see if we can get out of going to that. Wonder if we should tell them

Uncle Lenny is coming out of prison and going to be sleeping on the sofa for a few days? Hmm…better not – we're in enough trouble already. But what if one of the kids tells her? God, I wish the social worker was not coming around.

As you can see here, the parent also has a full agenda! It is easy to imagine this meeting going very badly. For instance, if the social worker comes in saying that they need to talk about the report and the teacher's concerns about Ezra, then it is easy to believe the parents will push back. Who could blame them? On the other hand, if the social worker simply follows the parents' 'agenda' and talks about practical help for flooding, then they would not be doing their job because they would not be addressing concerns about the child.

A top tip before entering any meeting (something that will sound very obvious when written down but is more complicated to achieve in practice) is to know, and perhaps write down, the things you would like to achieve in the meeting. This can be topics to discuss, or vaguer things, such as building a better relationship. One is always finding out what the family want to talk about. Then – and this is the really crucial bit – underline the ones that are absolutely essential. This should usually just be a couple, and at most three. (Sometimes there are no essential items. If that is the case, you might want to question whether the meeting is worth having?)

The point of this exercise is so that when the family comes with their agenda, and particularly when that involves a major unexpected development, in negotiating the focus of the meeting you can have a sense of what you need to talk about and what you can leave for another time. Less experienced workers often struggle with prioritising and make the mistake of overloading meetings – although even experienced workers sometimes do the same. This exercise can help you think through what to prioritise.

⦿ PAUSE AND CONSIDER…

Think about the next meeting you have planned. What topics do you want to discuss? Which of these are essential? What do you think the parents' agenda items might be? How can thinking about your agenda and that of the parents help you plan for the session?

So, for instance, in the above scenario if the social worker made such a list, their list might look like this:

- Contents of child protection report.

- Teacher's concerns about Ezra.

- Leak in living room.

- Change of conference time.

- Seeing Ezra alone.

- What do the parents want to discuss?

The concerns from the teacher may be the most pressing thing. The child protection conference report and change of time for the meeting could be discussed at another meeting if necessary, and if you saw Ezra alone last week, perhaps that is not essential today. But the concerns from the teacher are serious enough that you have to discuss them today no matter what else happens.

So, having thought about one's own agenda, and realised that the parents will have their own agenda, what is involved in negotiating an agreed agenda?

ADDRESSING THE CONTEXT

Most meetings happen in family homes (Ferguson 2010). As such, we are a professional guest. This is different from most MI contexts, and here we suggest some issues to consider in ensuring the home context is as useful as possible for a helpful meeting.

There are rules of politeness that we customarily observe when in somebody's home, such as checking where we should sit and deciding whether or not to accept the offer of a drink. However, as a professional – and perhaps particularly a professional who may have difficult things to say – we may need to ensure that the context for the conversation is appropriate. This is not something we usually need to do in an office meeting, and it is not generally a feature of counselling for that very reason. However, if we need to have a difficult conversation with somebody, we need to ensure the context is right. Common issues we may need to consider include:

- whether the TV or other source of noise is on

- whether children should be present

- if there are other people there, whether they should be present

- an aggressive or loud dog.

We need to make a decision about what seems appropriate – bearing in mind that we are a professional guest in somebody else's house. However, if we think it appropriate, simply asking politely is usually simplest. For example:

> Would it be OK if we switch off the TV?

Or:

> I think this might be a chat for just the grown-ups. Could Lena play in her room for a while?

Usually, people agree to such requests. If they do not, you need to make a decision about whether you can continue in a less-than-perfect situation. You may need to consider your own feeling of safety and the confidentiality of the conversation. While the situation may not be perfect, the parent is a collaborator, and their view on the context that they want to create is also important. An important consideration, however, is that they may not know what topics you plan to bring up. Once the context has been agreed, you can move on to the agenda of the meeting.

NEGOTIATING THE AGENDA

Agreeing an agenda is a key element of purposeful dialogue, and it is in theory relatively simple to do. Essentially, it involves three elements:

- letting people know what your agenda is – usually through an 'agenda-setting statement'

- eliciting from people what they want to discuss

- reviewing the two agendas and agreeing priorities.

An agenda-setting statement is best kept relatively short and then followed up with a question to elicit from others what they may want to discuss. So it could be as simple as:

> I know Leanne started secondary school last week, and I just want to find out how you and Leeanne feel it is going? Is there anything you would like us to talk about?

However, often it is a bit more complicated. When there are a few things to discuss, your aim should be to keep it relatively simple, and where possible to check that parents or others have understood your agenda and then for you to ask about their 'agenda' (meaning the things they want to talk about). So, with the Ezra example above, an agenda-setting statement might be:

> The main thing I want to talk about is how Ezra is doing at school. But I also wanted to talk about next week's meeting – and, of course, find out how you are doing and about the leak. If there's time, it would be great to have a chat with Ezra on his own. Is that OK? [Allow time for an answer and discussion: often just an assent or sometimes an introduction of their agenda.] What would you like to talk about?

Usually the parent adds one or two things and you may feel that you can manage to cover all the issues raised. More often, however, it will feel as if there is too much to discuss in one meeting and so you will need to prioritise.

The main challenge in reviewing and prioritising is making a decision about whether you need to direct, follow or guide – and not assuming that your agenda items are necessarily more important than the parent's, although sometimes they will be if you have specific concerns to discuss. Sometimes you can approach this in a classically MI way when you are guiding the parent to find focus but letting them make decisions about priorities. For instance, a guiding way might involve you saying something like this at the beginning of a meeting after each of you has said what you want to cover:

> Well, that is a lot for us to talk about. Of these things, what are the most important one or two for you?

This is guiding because it is shaping the scope of the discussion – identifying that just a couple of things should be discussed – but it is leaving the choice of these to the parent.

Sometimes the worker may need to be more directive, while allowing some scope for discussion. Such a comment might take the following form:

> That's quite a lot we could talk about. We probably won't have time to get through everything. For me, the most important thing is I need to talk about how Ezra is doing at school. What is the most important thing you would like us to talk about?

Sometimes the situation may mean that we need to be very directive, and there is not going to be a negotiation about what to talk about. The following is an example of agenda-setting in this kind of situation:

> I am afraid I am here to talk about a serious concern. We have had an allegation about Ellie being hit. What I would like to do is tell you what we have been told and then hear your point of view. So…

Here there is no negotiation of the agenda. The worker is setting out not just what needs to be discussed but also the rough framework for the discussion – namely, sharing of concerns and then hearing the parent's account. This is wholly appropriate; to pretend the parent can set or adjust this agenda would be disingenuous.

Agenda negotiation can happen at the beginning of a meeting, but actually it is at least as common *during* a meeting. For instance, you thought you could cover the issues, but after an unexpectedly long 40-minute discussion about something unexpected, you realise you have 20 minutes left and there are some key issues you still need to cover. At such times, you need to review the agenda and prioritise together, and as worker you may need to be quite directive.

The point is not that there is a 'right' way to set an agenda. Rather, we are striving to demonstrate that the skills of MI are the servants of the principles of the approach and the purpose of the interview. Knowing how to use a set of oars to row a boat does not mean you know where to go or guarantee you will arrive safely. Similarly, using open questions, affirmations, reflections and summaries (OARS) in MI can ensure you have more collaborative interviews, but by themselves they do not help you decide the purpose of such interviews. Rather, they are the tools which we can use flexibly and as appropriate to achieve our purposes. What is most important is that we bear in mind the key principles of MI when we talk with people. These include:

- treating people with respect

- seeking to understand their perspective/s

- trying to demonstrate our understanding of their perspective

- recognising that we cannot and should not impose change on people – that they must decide themselves what they wish to do.

RENEGOTIATING THE AGENDA

Setting the agenda at the start of a meeting is relatively straightforward. It is what might be expected, and when done skilfully, it is usually appreciated by everybody present, in the same way that a good chairperson clarifies what to expect in a group meeting. Renegotiating the agenda can be more difficult during a meeting – when, for instance, a discussion about something unexpectedly takes longer than anticipated and there is limited time left. If the unexpected discussion has come to a natural end, then it can be simply resetting the agenda for the time left:

> We've got just 20 minutes left, and a few things left still to cover. What is the most important thing that you want to talk about?

Yet it is rarely as simple as that. Two challenges in particular tend to raise themselves. One is ending a conversation about a topic – such as the unexpected issue that has dominated communication so far – and a second is imposing one's own agenda if that is necessary.

Ending a topic is very easy to do rudely. You could just say 'I don't want to talk about that, I need to talk about this.' Such a response is likely to create resistance and harm a relationship. The problem here is not that you are taking control, but that you are not showing you have understood what the person has been saying and why, and you are not negotiating what you want to discuss. Here, the MI skill of summary statements can be particularly useful when combined with some directive agenda-setting. For instance:

> It sounds like you are fed up about this water leak. You've called the council hundreds of times and they still haven't sorted it out and you are worried about the effect on the decoration and Ezra's asthma. From my point of view, you are doing the right thing and have got a plan to go down to the office to talk to the housing officer this afternoon. I'm going to back that up by phoning them to let them know how bad it is, as soon as I get back to the office.

This can then be followed by some agenda renegotiation. As at the start of a meeting, renegotiation of the agenda always happens on a spectrum of directiveness: at one end the parent can lead the conversation; at the other end you may feel that you must take a lead; but most conversations are somewhere in between. Agenda-setting following the above summary might, for instance, involve the following:

- Is it OK if we leave it at that and talk about something else?
- What else would you like to discuss?
- We've not got long before I go. And as I said before, I really need to talk with you about Ezra's school.
- I know the leak is a really important issue – but I know there are other important issues too. One that I really need to talk with you about is Ezra's school attendance.

There are an infinite number of responses – these just illustrate types of response on a broad range of directiveness. The key thing is to respectfully end one topic, indicating an understanding of the other person's perspective – showing them you understand – and then deciding the appropriate level of directiveness in choosing new topics. In light of that decision, you can negotiate how to spend the rest of the conversation.

It is worth noting that renegotiation often requires more directiveness than the initial agreement of the agenda – because time is limited and the usual reason for needing to do so is that your agenda has not been addressed. In our experience, this is one of the times when interviews that seemed to be going well can go wrong. The worker imposes their agenda and the parent can become annoyed by this. It is worth reflecting on this. In fact, if this is a difficult point, it probably indicates that the interview has been poorly managed for a while: the worker has been following, not structuring the interview sufficiently and running out of time. In addressing this, they move clumsily to direct the interview and the parent becomes understandably frustrated at the sudden change in approach.

There are a couple of considerations to avoid this. The first is that strategic management of the interview should be happening all the time. In the same way that a good driver simultaneously changes gears and avoids potholes while thinking about whether they are going in the right direction, so a good interviewer is using their listening skills but managing the overall flow of the interview and the timing of different elements. In doing so, they try to stop an interview being diverted off topic before it has become diverted. This is a challenging array of things to be doing at the same time. Trying to do them all can make people learning these skills feel that they have lost their 'natural' communication skills. This is a common feeling in becoming more skilled. The ultimate aim is for you to be so good at these higher-level skills that you can combine them with your 'natural' communication. And remember, we have all learnt our communication skills over many years; that is why we put the word 'natural' in quotation marks. In fact, communication is one of the most complicated skills we have as humans – something no other species can do in the way that we can – and in this book we are suggesting that to do social work well, we need to develop these skills to an even higher level.

The second consideration is the danger of 'over-steering'. Having allowed an interview to be dominated by a low-priority topic, the temptation may be to move to be very directive. The key here is to remember our MI principles – and in particular to show that we have listened and understood their point of view. Being directive always risks resistance. Sometimes this is a risk we have to take. The likelihood of resistance is reduced if we can demonstrate an understanding of the other's point of view, though there is no magic bullet or form of words that eliminates the likelihood of resistance. It just reduces the contribution that we are making to creating resistance by seeming to not understand or care what the other person thinks and feels.

AGREEING NEXT STEPS

A final common time when interviews run into problems is towards the end. At the end of an interview, we usually have to agree 'what happens next'. Sometimes this is very simple – for instance, because we are going to close the case or because all we need to agree is the time of the next meeting. However, usually this is rather more complicated, with some agreement about tasks to be negotiated.

In classic MI, the negotiation about next steps is started by the 'key question' (as outlined in Chapter 4). The key question is some version of 'What do you want to do about it?' The question serves two functions. It moves the talk from discussion of the problem to action, and it places the onus for deciding what to do with the person being helped.

Sometimes this may be a possible approach within children's services. Parents usually want the best for their children, and therefore after a really good discussion they are likely to make suggestions that are positive. Sometimes we simply need to support these suggestions. In a way that is consistent with normal MI practice, we would help parents elaborate on and make concrete and specific their suggestion. We might want to make it clear what they would do by when and agree a reviewing process.

Even in an MI counselling interview, it is often not as simple as this. Chapter 5 considered how and when we might give people advice. An option that is not usually open to the alcohol counsellor – though it is a common feature of not just child protection work but also probation, prison and other settings where the helpers are using MI in situations where they have power – is to raise concerns with a course of action. Raising concerns and managing power in very difficult conversations is the focus of the next chapter. Here we just need to note that raising concerns is best done in a conversation that is respectful, in which the worker seeks to understand and show understanding of the other's point of view, and where the use of authority is skilled and purposeful.

A final point to note is that in a conventional counselling situation the key question tends to focus on the person being counselled. In social work, we usually end meetings with both worker and parent having things to do. It is usually best to have a key question focused on what the parent plans to do. However, after this we can introduce what we – the workers – think we should do. Ideally, if all has gone well, the meeting should end with some actions agreed for one or both sides that can be reviewed at the next meeting. Agreeing these actions is a core element of the purpose of the dialogue in the meeting.

Conclusion

This chapter has moved beyond conventional MI to begin to think about authority and how to guide a meeting in child and family social work. It introduced the idea of purposeful dialogue as a central aim for partnership working, and then considered ways and points at which workers can manage an interview to achieve this. The concepts of a spectrum of directiveness, negotiated agenda-setting and the application of key MI skills at different points of the interview were explored.

Purposeful dialogue seeks to share perspectives and resolve them sufficiently to establish a plan with actions. This chapter has considered the management of such meetings and elements of a directive approach. However, it has not considered in depth a key element of the use of authority to achieve purposeful dialogue – and that is how we can raise concerns while staying true to MI principles. That important issue is at the heart of the next chapter, which considers using MI when there are very serious concerns about children.

Chapter 7

Talking about serious concerns and consequences

Chapter overview

Often workers tell us that they love MI but that they struggle to use it when there are serious child protection concerns. It is as if they have to leave aside MI when the going gets tough and revert to more normal practice. Normal practice often seems to be some version of 'telling people straight' – explaining concerns in a clear and unambiguous way.

'Telling people straight' – being open, honest and clear with people about concerns and the consequences of their actions – is a core element of child protection practice. People need to know where they stand and what is expected of them, including the professional's view of concerns and the likely actions we may take. This may seem like a million miles away from the gentle arts of engagement and helping that we have discussed in much of this book; no doubt this sense of disconnect is why so many practitioners struggle to use MI when raising concerns and explaining consequences. Yet there are numerous examples of MI being used successfully within child protection situations. For instance, when Galvani and Forrester (2011) reviewed social work approaches to substance misuse, they found that almost all the successful approaches in the field of child protection involved MI. What are rarer are detailed accounts of *how* MI can be used in serious child protection conversations. This chapter seeks to address this.

Of course, MI was not developed specifically for child protection conversations. Much of its development has been aimed at stopping workers diving in and prematurely or inappropriately telling people what their problems are or what they should do about them. This alone may be a useful contribution that MI can make to child and family work, as we often observe workers doing exactly this. Yet if that is all there is to our understanding of MI for child and family work, then it can at best make only a partial contribution; it would be no wonder that workers did not feel they could apply it to the most difficult conversations. Sometimes in child protection situations we have to tell people what we think the problems are and even what we think they should do about them. We think even the hardest conversations can and should be informed by MI principles, though they may need adaptation and interpretation for a child protection conversation.

This chapter builds on the previous chapter, which focused on the use of good authority and ways in which workers can direct the interview to ensure it is purposeful. In this chapter, we focus on raising concerns with families. We outline an approach that uses MI skills and principles to try to make the raising of concerns part of a dialogue with parents or others. Finally, much of the chapter focuses on a very serious child protection scenario and different approaches we might take to it, some more consistent with MI and others that are odds with it – either because they are too confrontational or because they fail to confront at all. We hope that by the end of the chapter you will understand how MI principles can and should be applied to difficult conversations in the work of children's services.

A helpful way of framing this is to consider how we manage two key things – the two Cs of:

- *Concerns* – how should we raise them?

- *Consequences* – how should we let people know what will happen if they do (or do not do) certain things?

Raising concerns and MI

Up to now, we have focused on the potential dangers of telling people what to do, and in particular emphasised its potential to create resistance. Yet even in counselling sometimes workers must be directive, and this is even more true in children's services. Consider the following example. While the quote is fictional, it is based on real people and situations we have worked with. Imagine you are a counsellor for a woman who says the following:

> Last night he beat me and stubbed out his cigarette on me. Last time I came to see you, he strangled me until I lost consciousness. This morning he said if I came to see you this afternoon, he would kill me. I'm sure he knows I'm here. But I'm scared if I don't go back, he will find me and kill me. So, what's the point? I might as well just go back.

The very real risks indicated here are far too serious for you to take a guiding role. A following role – listening some more – might be appropriate for a while, but ultimately we cannot simply listen: we need to respond honestly with our understanding of the situation. In the same way that if we see a child running into the road in front of traffic, we need to grab them first and then explain why later, so sometimes we need to move to a leading role in an interview – even if you are counselling. In this situation, we need to say clearly what we think, but to do so respectfully, and try to acknowledge that this woman has very difficult decisions to make. So, for instance, in response to the above we might say:

> What you have just told me is horrific. Nobody should be treated like that. What you decide to do is your choice, and I can see you feel pretty hopeless right now. I have to tell you what I think. I think you have come to the end of the road here. If you go home tonight, I think he may kill you. And if not tonight, then it will happen another night. You need to leave him. I also want to tell you I have worked with other women in situations like yours – women who thought they could not escape. They managed to escape and to rebuild their lives. I know that is a hard, hard thing to do… but what I think you are really telling me is that you know you need to leave him. And I would like to help you do that. What do you think?

The point here is that sometimes, even in counselling situations, we need to lead and be directive. The example given is of very serious concern, and it would be unethical to stand by and let this woman choose to go home, knowing the very serious harm that she could then experience, without expressing our views. Doing so would also show a lack of genuine care on our part. Being directive – saying very clearly what we think should happen – can and should be done in ways that respect the individual, the difficulties they are facing and their right to make decisions about their lives. The above example seeks to do this while being directive. Unskilled direction simply focuses on the worker's views and does not acknowledge those of the person being worked with. For instance, the worker might have said:

> That is terrible! You have to leave him! Going back is much too dangerous. You wait here, and I'll go and phone some refuges and find you somewhere else to stay.

The problem with this sort of directiveness is that it does not acknowledge the views and agency of the other. Ultimately, it is therefore more likely to create resistance, or superficial cooperation that does not last, and less likely to facilitate lasting change.

The need for directiveness is much more obvious and central in child protection than in counselling, because we also have the safety and wellbeing of the children to consider. Two principles in particular are important when raising concerns:

1. demonstrating understanding of the views of the other

2. emphasising agency and choice – the decisions people have to make.

We consider how these can be used in purposeful practice, and how they can help us move from raising concerns to purposeful dialogue.

Raising concerns and developing dialogue

Although MI does have some things to say about raising concerns, there is a crucially important difference between the types of concerns a counsellor or doctor might raise and the concerns we tend to raise in social work. In the former situations, we are firmly focused on what is best for the person we are talking to. In child and family work, our highest priority, legally and ethically, is the safety and wellbeing of the child, and often we are raising concerns about the behaviour of the parent. Sometimes we are doing more than simply raising concerns, as our concerns may have consequences attached.

This is a departure from MI as generally understood. Most of MI is about how to guide an interview so that it is helpful. In considering how to raise concerns and explain consequences, we are doing something beyond that. The way we think of this is that MI focuses on interviewing – which is how to facilitate a helpful conversation around behaviour change. In child protection work, we sometimes need to do interviewing, but the primary aim is to do something different to interviewing. As discussed in the previous chapter, we need to *facilitate a dialogue*. A dialogue is characterised by the *exchange* of perspectives, by interaction between points of view. To recap, this is different from most interviewing or counselling, because to have a dialogue the practitioner needs to be able to share their perspective. Our focus is how they can do so in a way that creates dialogue. We believe MI provides the techniques and principles for fostering dialogue.

Much of what follows involves techniques that workers may use to achieve a purposeful dialogue. These are often taken directly from MI and applied to more difficult conversations. Some are ways of thinking or approaching these conversations that are not part of the usual MI approach, but which share some of its key principles. The point we want to emphasise is that while much of the chapter considers the details – the techniques – we might use to raise concerns, these techniques are merely a means to an end. That end is to work in a way that is consistent with the principles that inform MI practice in child and family work.

The most important of these principles is that people should be treated with respect. A core component of this is recognising that parents and others we work with have responsibility for the decisions they make and their own behaviours. Related to this is the fact that we are each experts in our own lives; while a professional brings their own expertise, it can only be useful if it forms a partnership with the expertise each individual has in themselves and their circumstances.

Before considering the different elements involved in creating such a dialogue, it is worth reflecting on the nature of concerns, and in particular why raising concerns is so difficult.

Why is raising concerns so important and so difficult?

There is a real sense in which the ability to raise concerns is the central – the defining – skill of child protection work. We touched on this in an early work observing social workers, where we suggested that workers often enter the profession wanting to help people. This is a great motivation: it can help workers engage parents and children. Yet on its own it can be problematic. If this is our sole focus, we may fail to see harms to children, and we may be unable to raise the concerns we have about children with parents (Forrester *et al.* 2008d). Becoming competent in child protection work includes being able to identify and share with parents our concerns. The thinking in that article was inspired by the first author's experience as a social work student. See Box 7.1 for a description of a particular incident where in raising concerns he felt he genuinely became a social worker.

Box 7.1   DF's experience of becoming a social worker

DF was a final-year social work student and had been working with a family for some weeks. Each week when I saw them, their seven-year-old daughter would come and sit next to me or on my lap. She was a lovely girl – let's call her Jess – but she smelt fairly strongly of urine. Each week, I would go back and talk to my practice teacher and tell her this. Each week, she would tell me that I had to tell the parents. Yet I found it really hard to do so. It seemed rude – the sort of thing that we do not usually do in everyday life with people we do not know well. It seemed scary: the father was quite threatening and difficult. It was easy to imagine him becoming violent. And it was difficult to know how to do it.

Yet my practice teacher was right: the smell suggested some level of concern. Once recognised, I noted it down on file. Yet, as my practice teacher said, if something is noted on the file, the people involved deserve to know about it – both because we should strive to be transparent and because they deserve an opportunity to explain their perception. We eventually agreed that I would go with a more experienced social worker, but I would be the one to raise my concerns.

The meeting was tense for various reasons. Eventually, I screwed my courage to the sticking point – and it was really hard – and I blurted out something like 'And another thing I have to say is that the last few times I've visited, Jess has smelt of wee.'

All hell broke loose. The father jumped to his feet, shouting and coming towards me, looking as if he was about to hit me. I was only saved by the experienced social worker getting in the way and calming him down. There was lots of anger at a very young social worker, one who had not had kids and was judging the parents; and frustration that I had not raised any concerns before. But there were no doubt other things going on. Perhaps they felt shamed, upset and angered; perhaps worried about the consequences.

I have always felt that that was the moment when I became a

social worker – when I moved from simply wanting to help people, certainly very much wanting to be liked, to being prepared to say difficult things. The way I did it was very unskilled and probably unhelpful, and I have spent many years since struggling to find better ways of having such conversations.

We suggested in Forrester *et al.* (2008d) that there are three levels of skill in child and family social work practice. At the first level, we simply want to help people. The second level is characterised by more of a focus on the child and a willingness to raise concerns. It avoids the risks of collusion and failure to see risks that characterise the first level, but it can involve unskilled or even abusive practice, often with the justification of being 'child centred'. The third level – that of skilled practice – recognises that there is a vulnerable child *and* a potentially vulnerable adult who we are working with. It allows us to work with both child and parent/s, while recognising risks and potential harms to both. It is more difficult – because we are thinking about more than one person and sometimes balancing risks and harms – but it is the place where truly transformative practice happens. Focusing solely on the child rarely creates change in families, because parents are usually the people with problems, and they are also usually the people who have to make change happen. That is rarely the responsibility of the child (see Chapter 8). We therefore need to be able to engage and help them.

MI provides a way of thinking about how we might achieve this highest level of practice, by giving us skills and principles that allow respectful practice and help us move from raising concerns to having purposeful dialogue about how children might be kept safer.

HOW TO MOVE FROM RAISING CONCERNS TO PURPOSEFUL DIALOGUE

In applying these principles in difficult conversations such as those where there are child protection issues, our primary aim is to facilitate dialogue. The approach builds on the elicit–provide–elicit model, which tries to turn advice-giving into a conversation (see Chapter 5). Here we use similar principles to try to move from just raising concerns to creating a dialogue.

There are three parts to successful dialogue, each consisting of two elements. The three parts are obtaining the other's point of view (combining elements 1 and 2), presenting one's own (elements 3 and 4) and creating resolution (elements 5 and 6). The first two parts tend to form the bulk of a dialogue before moving on to the final part. The six elements are:

1. eliciting from the other their point of view

2. demonstrating an understanding of their point of view

3. being able to provide one's own point of view

4. checking their understanding of one's point of view

5. facilitating dialogue where there are differences

6. resolving differences – which can include agreeing to disagree.

These stages do not necessarily happen in this order. As discussed below, sometimes we need to raise our concern first, before hearing the perspective of the other. Indeed, as we note in discussing the question–concern trap below, sometimes it is much better to start by sharing concerns. The key point is that whatever order we work in our goal is to have a dialogue that leads to some sort of resolution.

WHERE TO START?

You can start dialogue by raising your point of view or eliciting the other person's. In general, presenting our own point of view first is more likely to create resistance – as the other person may feel we are imposing our perspective and not trying to hear theirs. However, where there are concerns, it can often be better to start by raising these, and the more serious they are, the more true this is. Indeed, if we are clear what we need to talk about, it is better to be transparent about that. To do otherwise can be counterproductive. For instance, in early work in this area that we did with simulated interviews using actors, we noted that to introduce concerns about a child's school attendance, workers would often use what we called the 'question–concern trap'. This took the form of an apparent question that was in fact not really a question. For instance:

Social worker: So, how is Jed doing at school?

Mother: Yeah, pretty well. He likes it and the teacher says he is doing good.

Social worker: Well, the school say he is missing a lot of school and they are quite worried about him.

There are a few problems with this approach. First, we did not get the impression that workers were necessarily very interested in what the parent had to say. They would ask the question but seem to pay little attention to the details of the reply. Second, the parent felt trapped. They had been asked to say something about school, and had said something positive, but were then immediately presented with negative information which led to rather difficult and unhelpful conversations.

If workers were not really interested in the answer to their question, why did they ask it? We think the answer is about topic selection. Deciding what to focus on in conversations can often be a tricky thing to do. Conversation analysts have studied in detail how we negotiate topics and changes of topic, in an effort to make it a shared activity. Asking a question is one of the most common everyday tactics for starting a new topic. Yet it is problematic if we are merely asking the question to raise the topic and are not interested in the answer. The workers knew they had to raise a difficult issue about school, and rather than simply saying what their concern was, they often used a question to introduce the topic, which then allowed them to share the concern. This did not work very well, because in everyday conversation we are interested in the answers to our questions, but in these interviews the workers were mainly interested in discussing a problem that the school had identified.

What seemed to work better was when workers were confident enough to identify the topic, raise the concern and then explore the parent's point of view. For instance:

> I've been in touch with the school. I'd like to let you know what they had to say and then hear what your point of view is. They said Jed is doing well when he is there, but that he is missing a lot of school – some weeks he is only in two or three days. How do you think Jed is doing at school?

The parent was still usually defensive, but they did not feel they had been trapped into saying everything was fine only to be shown it was not.

So what does good practice look like in the three parts of MI-informed purposeful dialogue?

Understanding the other's point of view

The skills we use here are essentially those of MI. In the first element, we ask for people's perspectives and explore their view through open questions and reflection. The second element is less common in everyday practice – in fact, we found it to be pretty rare – but it is an essential element of good practice: that we try to show people we understand their point of view, using reflections and summaries as appropriate. This creates a feedback loop that allows our understanding to be challenged. It is also important because a key source of resistance in interviews can be when people do not feel understood. This is much less likely to cause disruption to an interview if parents or others know that you understand what they are saying.

Explaining our point of view

The first element of this – how we should explain our perspective – has had comparatively little research or theorising devoted to it. This is in some ways surprising as it is a core element of child and family social work. However, there are some useful practical guides to good practice. Perhaps most useful are the insights provided from Signs of Safety and related strengths-based and solution-orientated perspectives (Turnell and Edwards 1999). These emphasise the importance of using clear, everyday language, being concrete and specific, and balancing strengths with concerns.

There is no magical form of words that provides the answer to how to raise concerns. Here we can identify some key considerations in doing this in a way that is consistent with MI. An important higher-level factor that helps is to establish early on in the relationship that you will raise concerns – that it is part of your role and indeed something positive. The interview presented in Chapter 6 provided some good examples of this – with the worker explaining that they will be open and honest with the mother. It can be useful at the beginning of the relationship (and sometimes thereafter) to explain what this might mean. A useful rule of thumb here is the one noted by DF's practice teacher (Box 7.1), which is that if you are going to write it down, you should usually tell people. This is partly about being transparent, but it is also because it gives them an opportunity to give an account of what happened.

So, for instance, near the beginning of the relationship you might say something like:

I try to be open and honest with families. That means if I am worried about something, I will always tell you. That's important because there shouldn't be any surprises for you – and because it gives you a chance to tell me your point of view. My basic rule is there should not be anything in our records that you don't know. If I am worried about something, I will always tell you – and that means I can also find out your point of view.

In systemic therapy, this is an example of a technique called 'warming the context'. This is essentially 'talking about talking' – making sure people understand the expectations around the conversation. This can also be useful when you know it is going to be a difficult interview or a difficult part of a conversation. You can warm the context by preparing people for bad news – something that doctors will often do. So, for instance, putting these together and applying them to the situation outlined in Box 7.1, perhaps it would have been better to have prepared them a bit. This would have been helped by some broader contextualising. So maybe:

> I know there is a lot going on, but I have something a bit difficult I need to talk to you about. I hope that is OK. When we first met, I said I would always be straight with you. I want to be straight about something I am a bit worried about – and I really want to know what you think about it. It is about Jess and the way she sometimes smells. She is a fantastic kid, but I think she sometimes smells of wee. I wondered if we could have a chat about that?

There is no guarantee that the father will not jump up and get threatening after hearing this, but it seems a much more sensitive and skilled way of introducing the topic. It warms the context – getting them ready for something a bit difficult – and emphasises wanting to talk with the parents; it tries to recognise their difficulties and any positives.

It is really important to emphasise that there is no form of words or therapeutic 'trick' to raising concerns. Rather, it is recognising that it is difficult but needs to be done, and then thinking carefully about the best way of doing so.

There are several issues to consider in deciding the best approach to raising concerns. One is how serious the concern is. A second is how sure you are about the nature of the problem. Each of these is a spectrum. This is very obvious for seriousness – a child missing school for one day is very different from a child missing it for a year, and there are of course many more serious concerns than that. The second spectrum – level of certainty – is a more difficult issue. Sometimes we may be confronted by something very obvious: a broken arm, missed school or missed appointments, for instance. Even here there can often be ambiguities, however. Was the broken arm definitely a non-accidental injury? If each parent denies it, how can we discover who caused it? Often the concern itself is a bit more ambiguous. For instance, the parent seems to be a bit slower than usual and is slurring their words. Are they drunk? On drugs? Perhaps there are lots of beer bottles all over the floor. Did the parent go on a 'bender' last night, or just have some friends around for a party?

A third issue is who is raising the concern. Is it you? For instance, you think you should raise the issue of the bottles or the fact the child smells of urine. And if it is you, are you raising a specific concern – such as these examples – or a concern about a pattern of events or behaviours that you have observed? For instance, do there always seem to be loads of bottles of alcohol when you visit? Or does the child always smell of urine? Often it is not the worker who is themselves concerned. For instance, perhaps a health visitor or neighbour or school has raised an issue that you as a worker need to broach with parents.

Thinking about where the concern is in relation to these issues can be useful in deciding how we raise it. A key consideration is how certain or tentative we think we should be. The more tentative we are, the less likely to create resistance, but if we are seriously concerned and fairly sure about a concern, then being tentative can be misleading. We need to be clear, though still in a way that encourages a response. For instance, consider the difference between:

> I'm a little worried that sometimes maybe Jess smells a bit of wee?

And:

> The last three times I've visited Jess has smelt of wee.

The former is less likely to elicit resistance, but it also risks the concern being swept under the carpet. The best response will depend on how certain we are and how serious our concerns are.

Checking their understanding and point of view

The key reason we raise concerns should be to facilitate a dialogue about those concerns. On its own, raising concerns achieves nothing – though perhaps it 'ticks a box' for the agency and the worker. So the key things to do following the raising of concerns is to elicit from parents their response to the concerns you have raised. Here the core skills of MI come into play – questions, reflections and summaries in particular.

Facilitating dialogue

The nature of the discussion can take many forms. Often the nature or impact of the concerns raised will be contested. Sometimes you will need to explain further what your concerns are or why you might be concerned about an issue. This process can take moments or hours, depending on the issues discussed, the different perspectives and the degree of disagreement. The nature of dialogue is that it is an iterative – repeating – process of information exchange and discussion, and this can take time.

However, ultimately it is necessary to bring the discussion phase towards some sort of conclusion. The approach to this is very similar to that outlined in management of an interview (Chapters 4 and 6) – summarising positions and then explicitly suggesting that the conversation moves on to agree what happens next.

Resolving disagreement

Moving towards resolving disagreement and agreeing next steps require a combination of summarising and agenda-setting skills. Central to this is identifying and making explicit what you agree on before moving on to areas of disagreement. It can be particularly helpful to highlight higher levels of agreement – for instance, you may both want the best for the children but disagree about how to achieve that. It is important to be explicit about this.

An insight from negotiation theory can be helpful here. Some negotiations are 'zero-sum' situations, in which there is a fixed amount of something, and if I get more of it, you get less. So, for instance, if I want to pay someone painting my house less and she wants to be paid more, then we each win and lose depending how much we agree on. Even in this situation, it is not as simple as this – I may also be interested in quality and reliability, and she may be interested in flexibility of working days and getting more work. Nonetheless, the core negotiation is a zero-sum one, where each pound I save is a pound less in her pocket. Often this is characterised in terms of cake – if the cake is a fixed size, then if I get more, she gets less.

In fact, most negotiations in life are not zero-sum. For instance, consider a husband and wife negotiating over childcare. The aim here is not just to get the other person to do more of it, but to ensure both people are happy with future arrangements – what is called a win-win situation. There is a sense in which the aim is to make the cake bigger so both people can have a larger slice. Thus, for instance, a couple might decide to pay someone else to care for the children, or to both job-share or work flexible hours. The aim is not just to get the other to do more (well, that should not be the aim); it is to negotiate an agreement that both parties are happy with. In a similar vein, in the vast majority of cases what the parent and the worker share is a concern for the best interests of the child. This provides the basis for negotiating an agreement which can be a win-win rather than a zero-sum game.

Dealing with very high-risk situations

The previous chapter and this one have considered how we might use the skills and principles of MI to turn child protection conversation into purposeful dialogue. At the heart of this was the idea of 'good authority', a version of social work that was authoritative, in that it combined care and power, compassion and authority. Authoritative social work also retains a focus on the child but combines this with a respectful and caring approach to working with parents. Here we consider how we might use these principles to deal with a very difficult interview.

The scenario we use to explore this is one we have often used in training. It is deliberately designed to be not just one in which there are very serious concerns, but also one where no matter what MI skills you use, the parent will not cooperate. The situation then becomes a test of how we can use MI in very difficult situations, with a non-cooperative parent and a child who must be seen. The scenario is loosely based on the final visit to Kimberley Carlile (Blom-Cooper 1987). Details can be found in Box 7.2. In a nutshell, Kimberley had experienced serious abuse and been severely injured. In a visit by a team manager, a very believable and intimidating father and mother convinced the manager that they could not wake up Kimberley because she was ill. Instead, the manager agreed to get on a chair, peer through a window above her bedroom and therefore missed what was probably the last chance to save Kimberley's life. While the scenario is loosely based on this situation, we have changed her name and other key details.

⏸ PAUSE AND CONSIDER...

Read the scenario in Box 7.2.

- How would you approach this interview?

- How might MI skills be helpful?

- What else might be helpful in having this conversation?

Box 7.2   The impossible role play

No matter how well the social worker approaches this role play, they will not be able to convince the parents to let them see Esme. The aim is not to see whether MI skills work; it is to test whether the skills can be used when you need to use court action and be very authoritative to protect a child.

Information for those playing workers

Two social workers are meeting with a mother and father following a referral from a neighbour that there have been 'piercing and distressing' screams from a child through the night.

The family has four children. The other three are in school/nursery. The second child – four-year-old Esme – is at home. There have been concerns around serious domestic violence from father to mother and physical abuse and neglect, particularly relating to Esme, over a period of some years. There has been a history of non-cooperation from the parents. Some workers have felt the father to be intimidating. On two other occasions when referrals of alleged physical injuries or neglect have been investigated, the parents have said they would cooperate – for instance, attending a GP appointment or a medical – and then not done so. In both instances, the case was closed because the concern was not sufficient on its own for child protection.

The case was closed two months ago, largely due to non-cooperation from the parents. It was decided that the threshold for legal action was not met and that despite high levels of concern nothing would be achieved through further work. However, the neighbour expressed very high levels of concern not just about the screams from Esme, but also because 'everyone knows' she is being mistreated.

In light of this, you have to see Esme today to carry out an investigation. Given concerns about the parents' failure to follow through on taking children to the GP previously, your manager has underlined that Esme needs to be seen today by you. This is non-negotiable.

The role play starts in the family living room with both parents present and two social workers.

Additional summary information for those playing the parents

Last night you (the father) lost it with Esme. You hit Esme regularly – she is covered in bruises. But last night you broke her arm and probably her leg too. She has been crying and screaming with pain. You have dosed her up with painkillers, and told her if she makes any noise or moves out of her bed while the workers are here, you will kill her.

Your plan is to get rid of the social workers. First, tell them Esme was really sick last night – stomach pains. You have given her some Calpol and she has just got off to sleep. You won't wake her up – would they if their child was sick and had just got off to sleep? If pushed, you will say you will take her to the doctor later when she wakes up. Second, if that does not work, you will tell the workers they can get on a stool and look in the window above Esme's bedroom door to see she is asleep in bed. Then you could take her to the GP when she wakes up.

In general, the father is threatening and tries to intimidate. The mother is terrified of him and tries to ingratiate herself with the social workers by being reasonable, explaining why they can't wake her now but will do later. A bit like a 'good cop/bad cop' routine with the aim together of getting the workers out of the house without seeing Esme.

Remembering these horrific situations is upsetting. Yet these are the stakes we are sometimes working with in child and family work. How on earth might we work in an MI way in such situations? Unlike previous chapters, the dialogue we quote was not recorded as part of our research.

It is hard to capture such very difficult conversations in practice, in part because they are fortunately very rare. Instead, the quotations we provide are a summary of different approaches we have observed in role-played training interviews using this scenario. We usually run it twice, once using some version of 'normal practice' and then asking workers to use MI – or demonstrating MI ourselves.

The conclusion of the role play is generally that the MI approach was just as clear about concerns, but that it was more engaging and respectful of parents. In particular, feedback from those playing parents tends to be that if the scenario had not been so extreme, they would have let the worker see Esme. This is really important feedback. Usually, a situation is not as serious as this. So how can we have difficult conversations while maximising the likelihood of cooperation where that is a possibility?

In our experience, there are many similarities between the 'normal practice' approach and that of MI. Both tend to start by explaining that the worker is there because of the serious concern, that given the history, they are taking this very seriously and need to see Esme. The parents then respond as suggested in the scenario by explaining the screams as Esme being very ill last night. She could not get to sleep, had a temperature and severe stomach pains; they gave her Calpol, and at last she is now asleep and they are not going to let the worker see her. There are then two main differences in the MI approach and that of 'normal practice'.

The first difference is that workers using an MI approach spend significant time trying to understand the parents' perspective and to show they understand it. They do the former through questions and the latter through reflections and summary statements. In contrast, normal practice provides what might be considered a superficial acknowledgement of the parental perspective and a move to use power.

So, for instance, a typical response to the parental account of illness would tend to be quite short:

> So, you're telling me she is ill, but I need to see her anyway. I'll be as quick as I can.

There are strengths to this approach. Most importantly, of course, it minimises the likelihood of Esme's harm being missed and maximises the chance she will be protected. However, there is no effort at understanding or sympathising with the parents' point of view. This may not matter in this scenario: we know the parents are lying. But usually, in such circumstances the parents will be telling the truth – or at least some element of the truth. And, in fact, if it was true that they have been looking after an ill child all night who is at last asleep, then it is easy to understand why they would not want them disturbed. One of the most difficult elements of child protection practice is that we often have to hold and believe the possibility of two things at once. In this instance, we hold in mind the possibility that Esme has been seriously hurt while simultaneously also holding in mind the possibility that she was ill and is now asleep. Our challenge is to engage the parents in a way that allows us to rule out one of the possibilities. How might we show more understanding of the parents' point of view? A typical MI response is more like this:

> You're fed up that we are here asking to see Esme. You have had a terrible night, Esme has just got to sleep and the last thing you want is for us to go in and wake her up. You feel we are always coming round, poking our noses in and making things worse. There is no way you are going to let us wake up Esme now. Is that a fair summary of how you are feeling?

This is – of course – an MI summary statement. Seeking to show an understanding of their perspective serves some key purposes. Most importantly, if people feel you have showed that you understand their point of view, they are less likely to keep making those points. It moves the conversation on, or at least makes it more likely that the conversation moves on. People may want to go back, repeat, elaborate or emphasise things they have said, but a summary tends to reduce people's need for that.

A summary statement and the listening that went before it are useful but they do not tackle the central issue of how the worker should use authority. Here it is worth returning to the example of 'normal practice' (quoted above) and considering a fairly typical next statement:

> I'm afraid I have to see her, because the concerns are too serious for me to leave the flat without seeing her.

A strength of the statement is that it is clear about the worker's position – there is nothing wrong with 'I'm afraid I have to see her.' However, the worker then says they will not leave the flat without seeing her. This is a statement that workers frequently make during this role play. There are two problems with this way of approaching the conversation. The first is that legally this is not justified. As a point of law, unless you had overwhelming evidence of immediate risk – for instance, a child screaming in pain in the next room or a parent incapacitated in front of you (in which case the common law of necessity applies) – you need legal sanction to follow through on this sort of issue. In practice, in the absence of that, you would need to involve the police to use their powers to investigate and, if necessary, protect. Second, while this is very assertive by the social worker, it leaves the parents nowhere to go. In a conversation in which the worker says 'I must see the child' and the parents say 'You cannot see the child', it is very likely there will be escalation. Violent or threatening behaviour are far more likely, and it is unlikely the parents will compromise.

Indeed, in our experience the normal approach to these role plays results in pretty short interviews. The worker says that they have to see the child, the parents get angry and the interview ends – often with shouting and unhappiness.

So how might an MI interview approach the conversation in a way that was clear about concerns and authoritative? There are two elements to this. One is to explain clearly what our concerns are and try to create a dialogue about it. The second is to explain consequences. Thus, for instance, following on from the summary above:

> **Father**: Yeah. It's just one thing after another with you lot. I mean, if your kid was asleep and sick, you wouldn't let some social worker wake them up would you?
>
> **Social worker**: The most important thing for you is that Esme gets some sleep and is not disturbed. I can see why you feel like that. For me, there are some other things I am worried about. I am here because a neighbour called and said she heard lots of screaming and it sounded like a child was in pain. Normally, in a situation like this we might talk about coming round later or taking Esme to the doctor. But a couple of times before when we agreed that with you, it did not happen. So I need to see Esme this morning to make sure she is safe and well.

The conversation then tends to spiral off in different directions. Maybe the neighbours hate them, and perhaps there are explanations the parents can give for why they did not follow through on seeing the doctor before. Once again, we need to simultaneously be open to the possibility of believing and not believing the parents; perhaps there is something in these accounts, but maybe they are a tissue of lies to cover up the fact that Esme is being seriously abused (see Box 7.3 for some thoughts on the broad issue of working with lies).

Box 7.3   Working with lies and 'disguised compliance'

In reviews of child deaths there is a heavy emphasis on social workers and others not being fooled by superficially plausible parents. This is sometimes called 'disguised compliance' – a term popularised after it was used in the review into the death of Peter Connelly to describe his mother's attempts to convince the worker there were no concerns. Does the use of MI imply that workers must believe whatever the parent says, and if so, does that not heighten the risk of missing 'disguised compliance'?

Some parents and other adults do lie to social workers, for all sorts of reasons. Most worryingly, adults who are deliberately harming children may lie to hide what they are doing, including serous criminals such as paedophiles and child traffickers. Second, even more parents will simply want to give the best impression of themselves – entirely understandably, when they are quite literally being judged (or assessed) by professionals. They may minimise or deny a problem to achieve this. Finally, parents may mislead social workers, without necessarily lying. This is particularly true for behaviour change – for instance, because they do not follow through on doing something they said they would.

So what does MI have to say about working with people who are lying? In a very important way, it has nothing specific to say. Sometimes you have to say difficult things to people. And telling a parent that you think they are not telling you the truth would definitely count as a difficult thing to say. The key thing in an MI approach is to try as much as possible to create a dialogue about your views. As we suggested previously, you can use the elicit–provide–elicit model to first show your understanding ('From your point of view, you are not hurting your child and even if you have hit them in the past, it never did them any harm'); then provide your point of view, using neutral and clear language ('I think that you do hit your child, especially when they are naughty and you are feeling angry. I do not think you mean to hurt them, but I believe that hitting them causes them physical pain, and makes them feel very afraid of you'); and then elicit again from the parent what they understand about your point of view ('What do you think about what I have said?'). Using an MI-based approach like this does not guarantee the parent will agree, or that they will suddenly 'confess' to having misled you in the past. It does make it more likely that your relationship with the parent will survive. Clearly, if you believe a parent is misleading you, intentionally or otherwise, you need to have a conversation with them about this. MI can help you have this conversation in a respectful way; it can help you understand why they might be misleading you (as an understandable thing to do). And, of course, we can expect resistance during the process of discussing lying. We should therefore raise lying as an issue only when we feel it is necessary. MI cannot help you to judge whether the parent is lying or misleading you in the first place, nor whether the lying is sufficiently important for you to make it a focus for discussion.

An MI-type conversation involves listening to these accounts, exploring and summarising them, but then coming back to the current situation. For instance:

> I guess this leaves us in a difficult situation. You do not want Esme woken up. You feel the neighbours hate you because you sometimes have loud parties, and their call is malicious and made up. And you say you tried to get to the doctors' those other times, but just ran a bit late and doing it did not seem important once Esme was a bit better.
>
> From my point of view, I still have this call we received, and the only way I can really find out whether Esme is OK is to see her and talk with her. We've talked for a while and I think I need to explain what your options are now. From my point of view, I have to see Esme this morning. What I hope is that you will have a think about it and let me see her now. But you do not have to do that. If I do leave without seeing her, you need to know what will happen next. I am so worried that I will call the police and have to come back with them. They have the legal right to make sure we can see Esme. Obviously, that is the last thing I want to do, but if you do not feel you can let me see her now, you need to know what would happen next...

Here again the worker is being very clear about their use of authority. It is perfectly possible that one or both parents would explode with anger and throw the worker out. However, the worker has minimised their contribution to such a response by (a) showing an understanding of the parents' expressed views and (b) explaining consequences. The parent may have very limited choices – 'Let me see Esme now or I leave and get a police officer' – but sometimes that is the reality of the situation. We have at least been clearer about the legal consequences of the courses of action open to them.

In practice, the parents are unlikely to simply take one of the options open to them. This is the point at which they might offer the worker the opportunity to stand on a stool and look through a window to 'see' Esme without disturbing her. Of course, that is not acceptable in this situation – and that would need to be explained clearly to the parents. For instance:

> I appreciate that you are really trying to think about how we can sort this out. But I have to be honest. I need to not just see Esme through a window, but also talk to her, and talk to her alone, to make sure she is OK.

The point of MI in this conversation is not that it will persuade the parent that they should let the worker see Esme. Given that Esme is seriously injured, there is no form of words that will allow that to happen. Rather, it is to do everything we can to treat parents with respect even in this difficult situation. Key to that are showing we understand their point of view and explaining clearly the limited options open to them. In our experience, the people playing the parents in this scenario find this approach far more difficult to deal with. A very confrontational worker is relatively easily dealt with through arguments and threats. A respectful but authoritative social worker makes non-cooperation more difficult. Crucially, if the scenario was not as serious as this is, the people playing parents tend to say they feel they would have cooperated with the worker. This is the ultimate aim in the fraught context of very difficult child protection conversations – to minimise our contribution to an already difficult exchange and maximise the opportunities for respectful dialogue and cooperation.

Emotions

Managing difficult interviews with comparative success is not just about technical skills. It is important that we also reflect on the emotional content of these meetings – for workers and parents (Ruch 2012). We have touched on these issues at various points in the book, but where the stakes are high, emotions can often be powerful and difficult to deal with (Ferguson 2005).

Parents may be feeling shame or stigma (Gibson 2014, 2019). They may be angry – perhaps because their parenting is being questioned, perhaps because they are being challenged about abuse or neglect, or because they have things to hide. Many will be scared that they may lose their child or have their family broken apart. These are powerful emotions, and we cannot do the work unless we recognise that our work is likely to trigger strong responses to such emotions.

Our own emotions may very well be very strong in this context. We may feel anxious or afraid. We may be angry – at the way we are being treated or the way a child is being treated. We may feel uncertain or lacking in confidence. We may not like a parent, or even a particular child. Plus, of course, other things may be going on in our lives that make us tired or less resilient than usual. It is important that we try to be honest with ourselves, that we seek help – from supervisors or trusted colleagues – to explore our emotions. Conversations such as these are very difficult, and we need to look after ourselves. As noted by Kinman and Grant (2010; Grant and Kinman 2012), when an aeroplane loses oxygen, you need to put your own mask on before looking after others. It is the same in this type of work: we need to look after ourselves and our own emotions if we are to effectively help others.

Conclusion

In this chapter, we have explored how MI principles and skills can be used to have very difficult conversations about child protection. A central concern has been how we can make such interactions into dialogues – where we do not just explain our concerns, but use the skills of MI to create a dialogue. Here, the listening skills of MI, and in particular reflections and summary statements, allow us to try to show we have understood the view of others. This is an important foundation for effective dialogue.

A second foundation is recognising that parents have both a right and a responsibility to make choices about their actions. To do this, they need to clearly understand consequences. We should not be telling people they have to do things, but explaining what will happen if they make particular choices. Again, this is likely to help us to create dialogue aimed at ensuring children are safe and cared for.

Yet it seems important to end with a note of caution. The types of skills and principles we have presented make it more likely we can create effective dialogue, and research shows they reduce resistance and build engagement. But they are not some sort of magic wand that makes people cooperate. These are difficult conversations, and it may be that whatever you say or however you say it, the parent does not engage or is hostile. The key thing here is that we need to be as sure as we reasonably can be that we have minimised any contribution that we may be making to creating these problems. If we do that, we have done all we reasonably can.

Chapter 8

Motivational interviewing and work with children and young people

Chapter overview

Child and family social workers aim to protect the rights of children. These include their rights to be heard, respected, kept safe and have their needs met. Our work with parents and other family members should be focused with this end in mind. Our direct relationships with children and young people are therefore likely to be very different to those we have with their parents and carers, while also sharing at least some similarities, such as treating them as experts in their own lives (Clark and Statham 2005).

Ironically, while many of us come into this work because we like working with children and young people, in practice most of our time is usually spent with adults (Ferguson 2017). Parents are responsible for the welfare of their children, and more often than not it is the parent or parents whose behaviour needs to change for a child to be safe. As a result, most of the chapters in this book focus on how MI can be used with adults, and we have gone into depth about how MI might be useful in supporting behaviour change and how the principles can be applied to difficult conversations. So, can MI be used with children and young people, and if so, how?

The answers to these questions are complicated. We consider them in two sections. The first outlines key elements of working well with children and young people more generally. We then suggest ways in which MI principles might inform and perhaps improve our practice in this area, though there is little research or theorising to guide us, so this is a rather exploratory section. We go on to consider MI as a way of supporting behaviour change with children and young people. For ethical and developmental reasons, we may often want to avoid asking children to change their behaviour. On the other hand, there are lots of behaviour-change issues that involve children directly and where MI might be a helpful approach. For example, if an adolescent has poor school attendance and we can use MI to help them improve their attendance, how would we go about doing so? The chapter considers an example of real social work practice and suggests ways in which MI might have led to an improved conversation.

Direct work with children and young people

Listening to children and forming relationships with them is at the heart of good child and family social work. It is necessary in order to understand their views and feelings, to assess their wellbeing and development, to explain what may happen to them and in numerous other ways. In all the countries of the United Kingdom, there is a legal expectation that we will obtain the views of children. It is a core part of showing that we respect and value them, that we are there to protect and help them, and that we want to understand them, their needs and aspirations. Without doing these things, we cannot do good social work.

There are many different contexts in which we will need to meet directly with a child. We may be trying to get to know them as part of an assessment or trying to explain something that is going to happen. We may be trying to find out what they think or want, or their perspective on a situation. Often our aim is simply to build a trusting relationship – including sometimes just having fun! And the meetings take place in many different places: in their bedrooms or front rooms, in cars or fast-food restaurants, in foster placements or at home, in the park or on a train. Some of our best memories of practice are about playing with children or going out to do enjoyable things together. One of the great things about social work is that it is very varied and there should be space to have fun and build relationships, particularly with children. And time spent doing this provides the foundation for a trusting relationship – something that is particularly important if it is necessary to have more difficult conversations at a later point.

Given the sheer variety of contexts and contacts we have with children and young people, we do not propose to present 'how to work with children' here. There are already some excellent books on this topic (e.g. Lefevre 2010). We also want to acknowledge that sometimes forming a positive relationship with a child is very difficult (Curtis *et al.* 2004), and much as we have said elsewhere, MI provides no magic solutions. Instead, we want to consider two more focused topics. One is how elements of MI may be useful for us in working with children and young people. The other is how and when we might use MI to help young people in relation to behaviour-change issues.

How might MI be helpful in working with children?

In any meeting with a child it is important to consider two issues:

- capacity
- context.

Children are developmentally immature. They do not have the capacity of adults to make decisions. This is true cognitively and physically, and it is reflected in law and policy. It is, in fact, one of the reasons why we need child and family social workers. Statutory social work is for those in society whose capacity to make decisions is for whatever reason limited in some way – including children and some adults with learning difficulties or mental health issues. In meeting a child, we need to have an understanding of child development in general and the specific needs of this particular child, and the ways in which they might influence their understanding and communication.

We also need to understand the context of the conversation. This includes the physical context. Where are we meeting? What would make them most comfortable? Would they be happy to meet the worker alone or with their carer? Would it be best to meet in their home or take them out? The context extends beyond the physical space in which the meeting takes place. It is also important to be clear in one's own mind about the purpose of the meeting. Is it to find out some information – for instance, what they think of their foster carer? To build a relationship? To explain something that may be about to happen? The purpose of the meeting will influence how we set it up and carry it out.

The principles of good work with children and young people have many similarities to good work with adults, but our practice often needs to be adapted to the developmental needs of the child. For instance, whereas with an adult we may talk about what is most important to them, with a five-year-old we might encourage them to draw and talk about their family. And while such a process might provide some insights into their feelings, we would not expect them to be able to give a coherent account of their feelings about their family.

This is obviously very skilled work, requiring a great deal of adaptation to the specifics of any particular interview. How might the principles and skills of MI that we have considered to date be helpful – or indeed unhelpful?

A key point to make is that the central principle that guides MI does not apply to working with children and young people. At the heart of MI is the idea that people can take responsibility for their decisions, that we should recognise this responsibility and work with it to support people in changing behaviour. This is, of course, not applicable to children. In fact, we are involved precisely because children and young people do not have full agency – full responsibility for the decisions they make. We consider later in the chapter what this means for how we might help them with behaviour-change issues. But this is a key difference.

While this means we are not generally 'doing MI' when we meet children and young people, some of the core skills of MI can be very useful when we work with them; for instance, in relation to each of the core skills.

OPEN QUESTIONS

The reason we use open questions with adults is to get them to talk – to share their perspective. The older a child is, the more likely that they will respond well to open questions. However, for many children open questions do not prompt them to talk. Instead, we need to use our knowledge of child development to think about more concrete and creative ways of communicating. This might involve, for instance, playing or drawing or prompts such as cards. Here the take-home message is that often what we want to achieve remains the same – that is, we want people to talk and we want to listen and understand. But our way of achieving this needs to be adapted to the child's needs.

AFFIRMATIONS

Affirmations are as important or perhaps even more important for children than for adults. So use them: search for positives and feed them back. The one difference is that praise tends to be more effective for children than for adults. The net result of this is that, on the whole, it is easier to give positive feedback to children. So, don't hold back – search for positives and tell the child what you have found!

REFLECTIONS

Perhaps surprisingly, reflections can be used with even very young children; however, they should be used wisely and with some caution. A reflection is, of course, your understanding of what a child or young person may be feeling or thinking. You need to be aware of the power differential between you and the young person and make it clear that you are trying to understand their point of view and encourage correction. For instance, you might comment to even a very young child on how they present or acts:

- You are smashing those cars around like you are really angry.
- It seems like you do not want to talk to me. You look really sad and unhappy.

SUMMARIES

In a similar way, summary statements can be used even with quite young children. And they provide an excellent opportunity to check with the child or young person that you have understood their point of view. For instance, even if you think the child you are talking with needs to stay in foster care, having listened to them you could say:

It seems to me you are fed up. You miss your mum and your friends, and you really wish you were still at the same school. That's why you smashed your room up and why you get so angry at school and sometimes hit the other children.

One difference is that it can be appropriate to offer a child sympathy. We caution against this with adults, but for a child it might be reasonable to then say:

If I were you, I think I would feel the same. I would feel angry, and perhaps sad and mixed-up inside too.

In a nutshell, MI has a lot to say about the core elements of good listening. Much of this can be applied to working with children, but as part of a broader consideration of how we work with children. We now turn to the heart of the section, which is a narrower focus on when we might use MI to help children around behaviour-change issues.

Should you use MI to help children and young people in relation to behaviour change?

In the classic 1993 film *Jurassic Park*, Ian Malcolm, played by Jeff Goldblum, who has been asked to review safety at the park, is – *spoiler alert* – attacked and nearly killed by a Tyrannosaurus rex. This would be enough to make anyone question the viability of cloning extinct dinosaurs for profit. Yet even before this unfortunate event, Dr Malcolm has already expressed his doubts about the venture. He says to the, owner of Jurassic Park, 'Your scientists were so preoccupied with whether or not they could, that they didn't stop to think if they *should.'* We need to ensure we do not make the same mistake with MI. Before we consider whether you *can* use MI with children and young people and *how*, we need to ask first whether we *should*.

To illustrate some of the complexities involved, we are going to imagine a relatively straightforward example – a 12-year-old boy with poor school attendance. We will discuss this example in order to illustrate four principles that we think must be applied to any use of MI with children (see Box 8.1). There are many more difficult scenarios we could have chosen where we might wish to focus on the behaviour of a child, such as criminal or sexual exploitation. Our aim here is to explore some of the complexities involved in thinking about behaviour change and work with children and young people. So, if we consider a 12-year-old with poor school attendance, should we use MI as a way of helping?

Box 8.1   Principles for using MI in behaviour-change discussions with children and young people

1. Critically reflect on the degree to which the child changing their behaviour is the right issue to focus on, considering context and capacity.

2. Be clear about who you think shares responsibility for the problem and be explicit with the young person that you do not hold them solely responsible.

3. Wherever possible, work with other adults to change the context and the behaviour of adults, and make sure the young person knows this is your approach.

4. If you decide to work on a problem behaviour directly with the child, be transparent about your agenda and preferred outcome.

We could certainly try. We could visit the young person and ask them a series of open questions to explore their views. We could show we were listening by using basic reflections, while seeking to focus on their ambivalence. We could use more complex reflections to highlight and reinforce examples of change talk and affirm their ability to make changes and succeed. Because we have a clear preference for what they should do (they should increase their school attendance), we would be able to strategically focus the conversation on that outcome. Such an approach would seem to have a reasonable chance of success and could be done without the need to be overly directive or authoritarian.

Yet it is worth thinking about this situation in greater depth. One key question is: who do we think is responsible for 'the problem' and would the young person changing their behaviour represent a suitable solution? By using MI skills to talk with the young person directly, we are implying that *he* is at least partly responsible for his own poor school attendance. And perhaps he is. Would we think the same about a 10-year-old? Or a 5-year-old? Even if we do think it is reasonable to ask a 12-year-old what he can do to improve his school attendance, few of us would think the same about a 5-year-old. And there is no clear defining line between when the child is too young and when they are old enough. Our judgement about this will also depend on the nature of the problem. A 12-year-old can be held responsible for keeping their bedroom tidy. They may be partly responsible, in some cases at least, for their own school attendance. They are absolutely not responsible for their parent's mental health problems or for being the victim of criminal or sexual exploitation.

In any situation, irrespective of 'the problem', we would normally aim to work with adults as well as children, most obviously parents and carers but other family members too, and other professionals such as teachers. Rarely would we aim to work solely with the child in relation to behaviour-change issues. Part of the reason why we treat children differently from adults is that we understand they do not have the moral, emotional or cognitive abilities to always discern right from wrong (depending on their age and level of understanding) or to plan and adjust their behaviour accordingly (ditto). One of the most important aspects of socialisation is to ensure that we, adults, help children to develop these sensibilities and abilities. When faced with a child whose behaviour seems problematic in some way, such as not going to school, we need to ask to what extent they are being supported by the adults around them. Are their parents willing and able to take an interest in what they are doing? Do they have adults around them whom they trust and can talk to? If not, it should be no surprise that they are experiencing 'behavioural problems'.

Returning to our 12-year-old with poor school attendance, we can review the principles covered so far. First, we have a clear agenda and a preferred outcome, and we can be transparent about this with the young person. Second, we do believe, at least to some extent, that the child could change his behaviour and that this would make a positive difference, even though we do not think he is wholly responsible for the problem. And third, we can work with adults as well as the young person, as part of our aim to make things better.

Having run through these principles, we decide to visit the boy at home and explain our thinking. We ask open questions and reflections to find out what the child thinks about school, the reasons for his poor attendance and what he wants to do about it. As we develop empathy, the young man tells us that he has been experiencing homophobic bullying and this has made him avoid school as much as possible. We considered above that we need to take account of context and history when deciding whether someone is or could be responsible for changing their behaviour in relation to the problem. Having now obtained some contextual information about the boy's school attendance, how does this affect our thinking? Obviously, we would not ask the young man what he thinks he might do to reduce the bullying behaviour. Victims are not responsible for the bullying they experience. We should not hold the victims of domestic violence responsible for the behaviour of the perpetrator (Devaney 2008), and the same applies to the victims of bullying and their bullies. It may be that we conclude instead that if we can work with the school to end the homophobic bullying, then our young man's school attendance is likely to improve without him having to do anything more. In this way, we demonstrate our third principle – that it is preferable, where possible, to ask adults to change their behaviour, rather than children and young people. If we are still of the view that some behaviour change on the part of the child would be helpful, then we may decide instead to focus on changing the context *and* the behaviour. Rarely will it be appropriate for the child's behaviour to be our sole focus in creating change.

These are not just theoretical considerations. For many years, services focused on the sexual or criminal exploitation of young people regarded them as responsible for their behaviour – indeed, their behaviour was considered to be the problem. This is an example of getting the focus wrong. The adults and social situations creating problems should usually be the focus for change, and our work with young people around behaviour change should at most be only one part of a response to problems (see Lefevre *et al.* 2017).

Can you use MI with children and young people?

Having considered the question of whether you should use MI with children and young people, we now turn to the question of whether or not you can. The short answer is yes. There are many examples of therapists, social workers, health professionals and others doing this. And many studies (mostly from healthcare settings) have been published which show that using MI with children is either more effective or no worse than providing care-as-usual.

Review of the evidence

Broadly speaking, there is no published empirical research in relation to the use of MI with children and young people in the specific context of child and family social work. A lot of the evidence we have relates to healthcare, and although there is some overlap in the kinds of problems encountered by healthcare professionals and those encountered by social workers, the context is different. Social workers generally exercise statutory powers over people for one (even though it may not always feel like that in day-to-day practice). Another difference is that while many parents will voluntarily take their child to see a healthcare professional, comparatively few parents would welcome the intervention of statutory social work services. As outlined above in relation to our four principles, we need to pay close attention to these differences when thinking about how best to use MI with children.

MI and child development

We also need to think about child development, and to acknowledge that it is often a gradual and non-linear process. While there is a clear legal divide between childhood and adulthood, no such clear line exists in developmental terms.

The question of cognitive development is an important one because MI is heavily reliant on the use of language. It requires that you and the other person can engage in a fairly high-level conversation about one or more problems. It requires that the person you are trying to help is able to think about the problem and about themselves from a number of different perspectives. They need to be able to hold more than one idea in mind at the same time, to separate long- and short-term goals and to organise their present behaviour in relation to future desired outcomes. With all that being said, it seems amazing that anyone can engage in an MI conversation, let alone a child. And yet, of course, all of these things are part and parcel of what for many people is normal cognitive development.

Based on these loose criteria, there is good reason to think that MI can be helpful for most children aged 12 and older but is probably less helpful for most younger children (Strait *et al.* 2012). By the age of 12, the majority of children will have developed the formal reasoning and self-appraisal abilities necessary to use MI. They will for the most part be capable of inhibiting their emotional responses – not entirely (who can?) but sufficiently to have a reasonable conversation about their behaviour. Children of this age and stage of development are also often capable of sufficient self-regulation to set themselves some goals and to have the self-control to achieve them. As development is not linear, it may even be a bit easier to use MI with a typical 12-year-old than with a typical 15-year-old, as impulsivity may actually increase during the early years of adolescence. Yet there is no 'one-size-fits-all' criterion. Most children do not follow the path of so-called normal development because the process is so individual, and that is before we even consider the issue of social and environmental influences. On the other hand, it is useful to have in mind that even with 'optimum development', most children under 12 are going to find it quite hard to engage with you in a conventional MI conversation and are therefore relatively unlikely to find it helpful. It is important to take into account the specific development and needs of each child, as they may vary, and of course each child is unique.

Applications to practice

We have cautioned about expecting children to change their behaviour. Yet in practice often social workers do precisely this. In our experience, when this is appropriate, using MI is more likely to be helpful than many conventional approaches that workers use. Consider this example from practice. In this scenario, the social worker is talking with a 16-year-old, whom we will call Jennifer, about her poor attendance at college. In some ways, it is not unlike our hypothetical example of a 12-year-old with poor school attendance – though, of course, there is a big difference between being 16 and being 12. In addition, the worker also refers to the young woman's girlfriend and some concerns about that relationship. The young woman's mother is also present:

> Social worker: OK. How about madam? [Said in a lighthearted way] What's happening with college?
>
> Young woman (Jennifer): Don't know.
>
> Social worker: When was the last time you went?
>
> Young woman: …
>
> Social worker: When did she last go?
>
> Mother: I think for about a month she hasn't been going at all.
>
> Social worker: What are you doing? Are you not bored, Jennifer? What are you doing in the daytime?
>
> Young woman: I go out.
>
> Social worker: You go out. Are you still seeing Beth?
>
> Young woman: Yeah.
>
> Social worker: How's that going?
>
> Young woman: All right. We argue a lot.
>
> Social worker [to mother]: Are you happy about that relationship?
>
> Mother: No, she's always hanging around her. No wonder she doesn't want to go college. I'm fighting with her, I've spoken to her – it makes no difference. Where we got the penalty for her [a fine for the young woman having not attended college], I'm on her back. She's screaming at me, and she does what she wants anyway; she don't listen.
>
> Social worker: We need you to go back to some sort of education, Jennifer. You're not trying hard enough.
>
> Young woman: Jesus, I called the number [for a college helpline]. She said she was going to call back and obviously you just said the woman has left, so obviously she's not there.
>
> Social worker: You have to call someone else.

Young woman: Who am I supposed to call?

Mother: I don't know, but I've got a penalty notice.

Young woman: How do you know it's for me?

Mother: It had your name on it.

Social worker: What I'm trying to arrange is a meeting to see how we can go forward with Jennifer, because I'm very concerned about her not having an education. I think, Jennifer, you should come.

Young woman: No.

Social worker: Why not? We could have the meeting here.

Young woman: I'll go out.

Mother: It's fine, Jennifer, I'll take the crap for you. I've lost count.

Social worker: Last time, Jennifer, we spoke about the penalty notice and you actually showed some sympathy with your parents having to pay the money.

Young woman: Yeah, I do.

Social worker: Then what's the issue with you not going to college? How come you're not going? Because you know what the consequences are.

Young woman: I don't like the course – it's boring.

Mother: Why can't you just go and sit there?

Young woman: OK, fine. Tell me the day and I'll come to your meeting.

What do think about the social worker's approach in this discussion? They clearly want the young person to attend college, and we can assume they have her best interests at heart. However, this interaction has probably not made it more likely that Jennifer will attend college. Why not?

⏸ PAUSE AND CONSIDER…

- What do you think the social worker is doing here that is likely to be unhelpful for Jennifer?

- Why do you think they are doing it?

- What might they do differently, using MI skills and principles?

How might we work in an MI-consistent way with Jennifer – and her mother? First, it is important to reflect on our four principles. It may well be reasonable to work with Jennifer about her college attendance, but we need to start by being clear what we are trying to achieve and why. It may seem obvious that 'Jennifer should go to college' – and that is certainly the position of the social worker, who knows the family well. Yet our actual aim is to help Jennifer achieve her potential. For most children, and therefore probably also Jennifer, going to school or college and working hard is part of that, but young people often experience difficulties that make this challenging. Sometimes a period off school may be what a child needs. Let us assume that, knowing Jennifer, we think going to college is important for her. We need to explain this to her, but then we need to focus on the main thing missing from this conversation: what does Jennifer think? We might begin to make clear our view while opening up a conversation about what Jennifer wants with a simple statement and question:

> Jennifer, it's really important to me that you attend college and that you enjoy it. What is important for you at the moment, and what do you think about college?

From here we would first use the OARS skills of MI (open questions, affirmations, reflections and summaries) to explore Jennifer's motivations and her situation. If appropriate, we might then explore the gap between what she might want and her behaviour. However, it is possible that in understanding her perspective we may recognise that other things need to change. Maybe the way she is taught is problematic, or the way she is treated, or perhaps she has special needs that have not been recognised. We should also be working with the adults around Jennifer to try to address the same problem, and letting Jennifer know that this is what we are doing.

A key issue here is that while we can use MI skills to understand and support behaviour change for children, it is rare for it to just be the child who needs to change behaviour. It is more likely that we will produce a mixture of changes that the child says they will make, along with tasks for parents, perhaps others and often yourself as worker.

Conclusion

This chapter has considered the use of MI in working with children and young people. We suggested that the skills of MI can be used with children in a variety of meetings. The focus of the chapter was then on using MI to support behaviour change in children and young people. Here we unpacked ethical and practical issues. MI can be used to help teenagers with behaviour-change issues; however, we need to be careful about framing the child's behaviour as the problem. Sometimes the behaviour of the child may be one element of the problem, but usually we will be working with carers and often other services to address problem behaviours. To help in thinking about when and how we might use MI to support behaviour change with young people, we outlined four principles, and these are worth reiterating here:

1. Critically reflect on the degree to which the child changing their behaviour is the issue to focus on, considering context and capacity.

2. Be clear about who you think shares responsibility for the problem and be explicit with the young person that you do not hold them solely responsible.

3. Wherever possible, work with other adults to change the context and the behaviour of adults, and make sure the young person knows this is your approach.

4. If you decide to work on a problem behaviour directly with the child, be transparent about your agenda and preferred outcome.

PART THREE

HOW CAN WE BECOME GOOD AT MI?

Chapter 9

How to improve your own MI skills

Chapter overview

In this chapter, we consider how you can develop your own MI skills and become a great MI practitioner. If you have already read this far, you have taken an important first step and learnt quite a lot about MI and how you might apply it into child and family work. This chapter considers how you can take the next steps and become really skilled at MI.

If you have had or can go on training in MI, then that is great. Good training in MI should help you understand the principles and practices of MI better. But there is bad and good news about training. The bad news is that, as with any skilled activity, training is not how you become good. From driving to playing the piano, complex skills – like those involved in any communication approach – can be taught in the classroom but can only really be learnt by trying them out in practice. Yet this is also positive news – you do not need to wait to be trained. There are lots of things you can do to improve your own MI skills aside from attending training. The creators of MI, William Miller and Stephen Rollnick, were not trained how to do it (who could have trained them?). They developed MI by practising and reflecting on their own practice. In this chapter, we offer suggestions about how you can do exactly the same, giving suggestions for ways in which you might improve your practice right now.

The stages of learning MI

Some people like to jump into the deep end and learn everything at once. For most of us, however, it is helpful to think about the different stages that might be involved in becoming good at something. We hope that an understanding of common stages in learning MI will help you in thinking about how to order and use the suggestions in the subsequent five sections of the chapter. It may be useful to think about eight stages in becoming a skilled MI worker, preceded by a 'stage zero' of *un*learning non-MI behaviours.

Unlearning non-MI behaviours

The first step, before starting on the 8 stages of learning MI, may be to unlearn some things you already do! When learning a skill, it is understandable to focus on, well, learning how to do new things. Just as important, however, can be knowing what current behaviours you need to unlearn. Unlearning practice that is inconsistent with MI is not always easy. Many non-MI-adherent ways of talking with people may have been in use for many years, and at times may have been (or appeared to be) effective. And if they *have* proven to be effective, you will need to think carefully about how you can integrate them with your new MI skills, rather than discard them entirely. The most common practices we have in mind are:

- telling people why or how they should change – persuading them

- prioritising information-gathering

- relying primarily on asking questions.

It may be helpful to assess your own practice. You can either do this by thinking how much you do these things, or even better by recording some practice and assessing it. We cover how to do this at the end of the chapter.

In general, the more experienced you are, the more likely you will have to unlearn or adapt some of your current practices. We tend to find that most students or people new to helping people are more of an 'open book'. Yet it is important to understand also the strengths that experience may bring. While experienced workers are more likely to have to 'unlearn' some of the behaviours noted above, they are often more comfortable at using authority and combining it with an MI approach.

The next eight stages

Alongside unlearning non-MI behaviours, Miller and Moyers (2006) suggest that becoming an expert in MI tends to progress through eight stages. Table 9.1 below sets out the stages for developing MI skill, with the skills developed early on being foundational for more advanced skills in the later stages. What this helps to show is the importance of not trying to walk before you can run. If you are very new to MI, then you will need to spend time first learning about how to use OARS (open questions, affirmations, reflections and summaries), before moving on to think about change talk. If you are already good at OARS and can recognise change talk, then you can move on to thinking about how to elicit change talk and roll with resistance. An easy and common way to get disheartened is to try to leap ahead to the later stages, before you have properly consolidated your expertise in the earlier ones.

Table 9.1   Eight stages in learning MI (Miller and Moyers 2006)

Stage	Description
1. Openness to MI	A willingness to entertain a client-centred perspective
2. OARS skills	Proficiency in the basic client-centred skills, especially accurate empathy
3. Recognising and reinforcing change talk	The ability to notice change talk when it occurs and respond to it accordingly
4. Eliciting and strengthening change talk	An intentional effort to elicit change talk and reinforce it
5. Rolling with resistance	The avoidance of direct refutation of the client's arguments against change
6. Developing a change plan	Recognition of the right time to switch from discussing motivation to the formulation of a change plan, while remaining client-centred
7. Consolidating client commitment	The ability to notice, elicit and reinforce commitment-to-change language
8. Switching between MI and other approaches	The ability to combine MI with other approaches, and to switch between MI and other approaches as needed

So how might we progress to become a skilled practitioner? The next five sections consider how we might develop our skills in relation to the stages above, at whatever level we are starting from.

PRACTISING – AT WORK AND OUTSIDE WORK
Unfortunately, there are no shortcuts to becoming really great at MI. It takes a lot of practice. If you want to learn to play the piano, most of your time should be spent actually playing the piano (rather than reading about

it or going to lessons/training sessions). The same is true for MI. Here, we outline some activities that you can use to help make sure you get as much practice as possible.

The first suggestion is that practice does not always need to be with people we work with. Most of the skills we use in MI can be used in listening to anybody – and in our experience people love being listened to and heard! So it can be helpful to practise listening skills with friends and family. This can be as simple as trying to use the odd reflection (peppering them into our conversations) through to agreeing with a friend or partner that once or twice a week you are going to really listen to them. Maybe a friend has a problem – such as wanting to become fitter or lose weight – and you can agree that you will try to listen to them as carefully as possible using your MI skills. Whatever you are doing, the aim is for it to feel natural and the person you are doing it with not to feel there is anything odd about the way you are talking to them. Put another way, your aim is to 'own' MI so you can use it in a natural way that is *your way* of doing MI.

Next, of course, most of us have the opportunity to practise with children and families. Yet this can be overwhelming. Often when people leave training, they are very keen to 'do' MI, and they want to try it on their families, but there are so many skills to practise, and so many other things going on, that they fall back into their normal habits of practice. Here the situation is very similar to someone who wants to get fit. Imagine you see a programme that convinces you that you need to become much more fit. You may decide to start exercising twice a day, radically change your diet, get more sleep and drink less. That is a lot of change all at once, and as a result there is a high chance it will just be too much. What tends to be more successful is a series of gradual and structured change – like the NHS's 'Couch to 5K' programme, which builds up activity and fitness over a number of weeks. In a similar way, rather than simply deciding to 'do MI' with everyone, it is likely to be more helpful to focus on stages of skill development and try to master them one at a time before incorporating the next one. Some people also find it works to focus on one or two families, preparing and building skills with them in a systematic way and then thinking about how to transfer it to other families until it becomes the way they practice.

REFLECTING
Practising is one thing, but contrary to the saying, it does not always lead to perfection. Consider driving. Many of us drive for many years, constantly

practising the skills of driving, but do we get better? For most people, there is a steep initial learning curve but then we plateau out and more driving does not increase our skills. In sports coaching, it is sometimes said that practice does not make perfect – it makes permanent. What this means is that if you keep doing the same thing, then that will become your habit. So how can we do our practice in ways that will help us become better – that will make our driving more like the next Lewis Hamilton? A key thing here is that we need to introduce feedback, so that we are constantly understanding what we are doing well and what we need to improve. Feedback and how we use it is the key to improving our practice skills.

So how do we know if we are doing well? Or whether we could do better? Fortunately, there is always someone in the room, and they are constantly giving us feedback. They are like a personal coach, and if we learn to listen to them, they can help us become great workers. Who is this person? They are the people we are working with. In a previous edition of the Miller and Rollnick textbook on MI, the authors ended by suggesting that they developed MI once they realised that people were constantly giving them feedback during conversations. Resistance of all sorts was like a red light: danger, warning, be careful and (probably more than anything else) stop and try something else! In contrast, change talk was the green light: we are hitting the spot, this is working, people are engaged – keep going!

Understanding resistance and change talk, recognising them and being able to respond effectively to the feedback that they are giving you are probably the most important steps you can take towards becoming a skilled MI worker. Once you understand this constant feedback, then you literally never stop learning MI. You can use it during sessions and you can think about it after a session.

One helpful way of conceptualising this is through Schön's ideas of reflection-in-action and reflection-on-action (Schön 1983). The constant feedback during conversations allows you to reflect on what is happening, why you might be encountering resistance or eliciting change talk, and what actions you might take to change direction. This is reflection-in-action. In contrast, reflection-on-action is something we usually do after a meeting, and it often takes a more holistic view of what happened. For instance, why did that meeting go well or go badly? What was my contribution to that outcome? What might I have done differently? A skilled professional is able to reflect both in- and on-action, and both provide opportunities to improve our MI skills.

RECORDING AND LISTENING TO YOUR OWN PRACTICE

The power of reflection is amplified if we have an opportunity to stop and think about what we did, why we did it and what we might have done differently. A powerful aid to this that we have used ourselves and supported others to use is recording meetings and then listening back to them.

In theory, it is relatively simple to get an audio-recording of yourself in practice. Any modern mobile phone will have the ability to audio-record a conversation, either with pre-installed apps or by using any number of free downloadable apps. At the start of the interview, simply place your mobile phone somewhere in between the speakers, and hit record. Actually, recording a social work interview is more complicated than this. You will need to consider some key issues. The most important are, first, that you have the agreement of the participants, and that this agreement is based on a full understanding of what is being asked and that they feel able to disagree. The latter is a particular challenge. Often the people we work with feel relatively powerless and they may wish to please you as social worker. You need to think carefully about the relationship and be confident that the family members do not feel in any way obligated to allow a recording. Second, you need to ensure that the recording is kept secure and cannot be accessed by others. This includes immediate security, and a clear plan for what you will do after you have listened to it – that is, secure destruction. Finally, you need to think through tricky scenarios. One of these might be if the recording contains evidence of a crime. What would you do if the person admitted to hitting someone or dealing drugs? Worse still, what if they actually hit their child while being recorded? You need to know how you would deal with these issues, but you also need them to know when they give consent. They may also want to know whether they can have a copy.

These are challenging issues. When doing research, we deal with them by providing information sheets and consent forms to cover these eventualities. You will also need to ensure your manager knows about and supports your plans.

Given these challenges, we understand that only the most committed practitioners are likely to record practice and listen back to the recordings. That is unfortunate, as listening back to recordings is probably the most powerful single learning opportunity that there is. On the other hand, we are aware of local authorities and social work courses that encourage recording of practice to support skills development. This sort of institutional support for listening back to recordings is enormously helpful to develop cultures of reflective skills development.

Once you have a recording, you can listen back to it and think about your MI skills. You can do this in a relatively open-ended way, or you can use a framework for coding your practice. Both of these approaches have advantages and disadvantages.

OPEN-ENDED LISTENING

If you are just starting out, it is easier to listen back in an open-ended way. This means simply listening back to the recording while having two or three questions in mind, as follows:

- What sort of things do I say that sound most helpful?

- How does the other person respond to what I say?

- What sorts of things could I aim to say more or less of in future sessions?

If you are taking an open-ended approach, you probably do not need to do much more than this. However, once you have done this a few times, you may find diminishing returns in terms of how helpful this is for your development of MI skills. You may be ready for a more fine-grained and challenging approach to listening to your own practice. For this, a framework for coding MI skills may be helpful.

CODING YOUR OWN PRACTICE

There are various coding frameworks available for assessing MI skill levels. In fact, a recent review found 11 different approaches to coding (Manuel *et al.* 2012). The reason for this number of schemes is that they are developed in different contexts and for different purposes. Most focus on the behaviour and attributes of the worker, some also code the response of the person being worked with, and a few are simplified coding schemes. Many were developed for research purposes – to allow the exploration of how MI works or whether it is being delivered to a high standard. Several were also developed to support workers and supervisors in improving MI skills.

In our research programme, we developed a specific approach to coding for MI skills. We built this on an earlier version of perhaps the most widely used coding scheme, the Motivational Interviewing Treatment

Integrity (MITI) codes. We used four of the key skill areas from the MITI. These were:

1. empathy (demonstrating understanding)

2. autonomy (amplifying decision-making autonomy)

3. collaboration (working alongside)

4. evocation (eliciting intrinsic motivations).

Yet, as considered throughout this book but particularly in Chapters 6, 7 and 8, we thought that MI needed to be adapted for use in child and family work. We therefore developed three additional codes for use in this setting. We developed these through a review of the literature, a series of focus groups and a process of trial and error in refining the codes. These three skill areas were:

1. focus on child

2. clarity about concerns

3. purposefulness.

Our understanding of these elements of the role was based on MI principles – in other words, it was consistent with the vision of MI for child and family work that we have outlined in this book. We borrowed the structure of the MITI for coding these areas, creating a five-point scale for each, with a 5 being very highly skilled practice, 3 being an anchor point and 1 being very non-MI-consistent practice. Scores of 1 tended to be authoritarian, with the worker telling the parents what to do a lot.

We have researched extensively with these seven codes, rating hundreds of real interviews and a similar number of simulated interviews. A couple of key findings are worth noting. First, the seven areas grouped into three key dimensions of practice. These were:

1. care and engagement (empathy, collaboration and autonomy)

2. good authority (focus on child, clarity about concerns and purposefulness: the three additional codes for child and family settings)

3. behaviour change (evocation).

Our sense is that the combination of skills provides a fairly good description of the underlying dimension of practice for the first two of these. In other words, 'care and engagement' skills are well captured by empathy, collaboration and autonomy, and 'good authority' is well described by a focus on the child, clarity about concerns and purposefulness in the interview. We have a feeling that more work is needed on how workers support behaviour change, though measuring evocation is a good start for this.

Although this coding scheme is very much a work in progress, our findings do suggest it may be useful. We found, for instance, positive changes in practice as local authorities implemented change programmes, and were able to identify the positive impact of training and supervision on practice. More importantly, we found correlations between these skills and outcomes for families (Forrester, *et al.* 2019). This is important because to our knowledge this is the only evidence about the relationship between skills and outcomes in frontline child and family work. It therefore provides an important element of the rationale for the whole approach we present in this book.

We provide a freely accessible version of the coding scheme we use, with considerable detail on the CASCADE Centre website at Cardiff University (https://cascadewales.org). We called it the Social Work and Interviewing Motivationally (SWIM) code; however, the structure and much of the content is based on a previous version of the MITI so we remain indebted to Miller, Moyers and others. We also provide some guidance on how we use it, and the challenges of becoming good at coding.

Developing reliable coding takes ages. When doing research, we go through a painstaking process of developing and checking skills using recordings of simulated and then real practice. You will not be able to develop this level of reliability. However, we are not suggesting here that you use it for research purposes. To develop your own skills, the contribution that coding your own practice – or indeed that of others – can make is rather to provide a more fine-grained space for critical thinking about your own practice. For this purpose, any coding scheme can be helpful, as it will provide a detailed account of what key elements of very skilled practice look and sound like.

In coding yourself to develop your MI skill level, we suggest you do use the following stages:

1. Listen to the whole recording once or twice, usually taking notes as you go but not stopping the recording.

2. Being as honest with yourself as possible, try to give yourself the mark that best represents how you think you did in the interview.

3. Holistically, thinking about the interview as a whole: what do you think you could have done differently? In particular, you may find it helpful to consider whether (a) you missed particular key points in the interview to do something differently and/or (b) there were general things you could have done differently across the interview.

4. Based on this analysis, choose a short part of the interview – maybe just five minutes – to analyse in depth. Playing/stopping and thinking about what you said, why you said it and what you might have said differently.

5. Decide and write down some key learning points and actions for future interviews.

In addition, if you are able to listen to elements of the recording with your practice educator or line manager, this provides an exceptional learning opportunity. If you are able to do this regularly – say once a month – your practice will improve substantially.

Conclusion

This chapter has considered how you might help yourself become better at MI. The focus has been on moving beyond thinking that training is the answer, to considering ways you can build reflection and learning into your everyday practice. To do so, it is worth thinking about the nine stages of learning MI. We then considered the importance of practice and opportunities to do so, reflection on and in practice, the feedback those we work with constantly give us, and the potential that recording practice and possibly coding ourselves present for improving our skills.

The next chapter considers how you might help others become better at MI. In fact, one of the best ways of improving your own knowledge and skills is to teach them to others . As several people have said, 'If you really want to understand something, try to teach it to someone else.'

The key lesson of the chapter is really that there is no secret to MI, no expert who can tell you the 'secrets' – the secret is for you to be committed to becoming a better practitioner and using every opportunity you can to become better. It is rather like becoming the Dragon Warrior in *Kung Fu Panda* (warning: spoilers ahead…). The Dragon Scroll is just a mirror – because there is no secret ingredient. We each hold within us the potential to be the 'Dragon Social Worker'. We just need to be dedicated to becoming the best worker we possibly can be.

Chapter 10

How to help others develop MI skills

Chapter overview

This chapter considers how we can help others become better at MI. It starts by examining improving practice as a form of behaviour change, and the lessons that MI may therefore have for learning MI itself. It then reviews key opportunities to help people improve their skills, including training, supervision and coaching. Our intention is that the chapter will be useful for those with some responsibility for improving the practice of others, including trainers, line managers, practice educators and senior managers. However, because the theme of the chapter is about how we learn skills, we hope it will have insights and lessons for anyone interested in becoming better at MI – or indeed at social work practice more generally.

Learning MI as a form of behaviour change

It is often noted within the MI community that changing practice is itself a form of behaviour change. It is therefore suggested that the principles of MI may be useful for understanding how we help people change their practice. Considering learning MI in this way provides important insights, but it also has some limitations. These limitations have implications well beyond learning MI – they apply to helping people in general.

What insights can MI provide into learning MI?

The key insight MI provides for all learning is that we should pay attention to people's motivations. Indeed, we can go further: maximising people's motivation to learn is more important than teaching them how to 'do MI'.

Providing training or other input for people who are not keen to learn will achieve little. Conversely, if people are convinced that the principles and skills of MI are how they want to practise, then they will often learn themselves. This concept is pithily captured in one of our favourite quotes, which is believed to be from Antoine de Saint-Exupéry (though the source is uncertain):

> When you want to build a ship, do not begin by gathering wood, cutting boards, and distributing work, but rather awaken within people a desire for the vast and endless sea.

Similarly, with helping people get better at MI, do not start with the technical work of training in skills or feeding back on practice. The first task is to evoke from people a passion for MI. How might this be done?

MI conceptualises motivation as the gap between the life we are living and the life we want to live. This is often about fundamental values, about what we think is important. Similarly, for social workers and other professionals the key question is this: are you completely happy with your practice? Is there a gap between the way you are currently practising and how you would like to be working?

If the honest and thoughtful answer to this is that there is no gap, then there is little point trying to change people's practice. They are perfectly happy with it, so why would they strive for anything different? Yet in our experience, workers are rarely completely happy with their practice. There are lots of reasons for this. Social workers are a relatively modest bunch and usually want to be better at helping people. Furthermore, they are often acutely aware that their own practice is not as good as they would like it to be. This is partly because of the everyday pressures that they work under, which mean that they feel they do not have time to work with people as they would like to. At a deeper level, the system they are part of has all too often shaped their practice to be far from the type of work they came into the service to deliver. The focus on risk and challenge has often squeezed out the space for compassion and respectful interaction. In our experience, social workers and social work students are usually hungry for an approach such as MI – or for others that emphasise developing skills in working better with people.

The primary contribution of MI is therefore that it generally provides a better vision of how to do our work than 'normal service'. This is rooted in three things about MI:

1. *Its values and principles*

   The compassionate nature of MI, and the respectful attitude it has to individual autonomy and decision-making, are a good fit for social work and related disciplines. They are usually the sorts of values and principles that brought us into this type of work.

2. *Its theory and practices*

   Often workers and students want to help people but do not really have a theory about how to do it or why this is often so difficult. MI provides a theory that can help us understand why people are not changing and provides lots of guidance for how we can improve our practice.

3. *Its evidence base*

   A key feature of MI is that it has a very strong evidence base. This is often not considered important in our sector. Several of the most popular approaches to practice have little or no evidence that they work. In contrast, there is a huge body of evidence for MI, albeit largely in other settings. We find this an attractive feature of MI, not because it provides some sort of 'proof' that MI works but because it allows us to have a rounded understanding of the strengths and limitations of MI: while the body of evidence suggests MI tends to work, it also highlights that it does not always work and that delivering it to a high standard is deceptively difficult. We are drawn to a method with an evidence base both because the evidence justifies the method *and* because it allows us to understand the limitations of MI. In a nutshell, we are wary of methods that over-claim their impacts (see Box 10.1 for a fuller discussion).

Box 10.1   MI and other methods, approaches and frameworks

The last 15 years have seen a substantial increase in applying different frameworks of practice to child and family social work. Signs of Safety emerged in Australia in the 1980s but has become far more popular in the UK over this time period. Restorative approaches have been adapted from criminal justice settings.

Systemic practice and MI have been used as the basis for both whole systems change and the training of social work students. More recently, trauma-informed practice has become popular. How do these different approaches relate to one another – and do we think MI is the best one?

In our opinion, in practice most of these approaches have more in common than differences. Their values tend to be similar – for instance, respect, compassion, collaboration and a focus on strengths. Their practices are also similar. This is probably because helping people probably has common core elements, whatever theoretical orientation it starts from. It may also be because these types of values are what social work seems to need now. There are also a lot of similarities in the recognition that delivering such methods requires organisational change and multiple supports for improving practice.

We consider the debate about which method is best as akin to asking whether the saxophone or the piano is better. We can have our preferences, but more important is becoming good at using the instrument we choose. A good saxophonist or pianist can play music well. Someone who does not practise and receive feedback is not likely to be able to play any tune. Helping people is like music: being good at helping people is less about what model you prefer than becoming good at the approach you choose to focus on. We are also of the view that it is probably beneficial to focus on getting very good at one or two instruments, rather than trying to become merely competent at so many instruments that you simply do not have time to master any of them.

Taken together, we feel that these three things provide a compelling vision for why MI may be a good thing for workers to become skilled in – though we tend to find most workers are far more interested in the first two. What are the implications for how we might support people to become more skilled?

The most important lesson is that we need to evoke from people their own motivation. How might we do this? As in working with an individual, this is not about 'tricking' people into becoming motivated. It is about allowing them to explore whether there is a difference between how they would like to work and how they currently practise. There is no one way to do this – and we would encourage you to think creatively about how to do this in training or whatever context you are supporting the development of MI. However, here are the types of questions you might want to help people to explore:

- Why did people come into this work?

- What are their core principles and drives for sticking to the work?

- What sort of practitioner do they want to be?

- What is the best practice they have observed? What was so good about it?

- What is the very best practice that they have done? A meeting they were really proud of?

- Can they think of families or children for whom things have gone really well, and what kind of practice helped support these positive outcomes?

- Are they completely happy with their current practice?

- What theories inform their practice? In particular, how do they think they help people by talking to them? It is often worth unpacking people's thinking here – much current practice does not have a theory about how it 'works'.

- If they woke up tomorrow and turned into the best worker they could possibly be, what difference would families see?

Questions such as these can be covered through small groups or individuals considering them directly. But it tends to work better when we vary our mode of presentation. So tasks might include not just small group discussions but:

- reflecting on videos or recordings

- case studies – for instance, how would you approach this on a good day? On a really bad day?

- role plays.

Many other resources are available on https://motivationalinterviewing.org.

The point is to try to be clear what we want to evoke, which is most usefully done by thinking about evocative questions. We then need to be creative in thinking about the different ways we can get people to explore such issues.

MI provides a very helpful insight that applies to training for any type of practice. This is that it is more important to address motivation than to 'teach' people. Once motivated, people take responsibility for their own learning. Without motivation, even great teaching will make no difference. MI also provides a useful framework for thinking about what motivation is – the motivational gap – and how we might focus on it. In addition, the international community of MI trainers have amassed a huge store of creative and interesting ways to deliver training, and they share most of these freely at the motivationalinterviewing.org website. There are lots of resources you can tap into to explore how to train people, including some we identify in the Further Resources section.

What are the limitations of MI as a way of thinking about skills development?

In our experience, if you follow the principles in the section above, groups of workers tend to be very motivated to learn MI. It is also possible to help them define a type of good practice that has many similarities to MI – in that it is respectful, empathic and purposeful. Yet you cannot treat a training session as if it were a session of MI counselling, for two reasons. The first is that people do not necessarily know what MI is. While they have many strengths and we should recognise these existing strengths, training and other input is in part required because there are lots of things they do not know, or do not know how to do. However good you are at facilitating discussions, it is unlikely that any group could 'invent' MI-adherent practice simply through elicitation. There is therefore a clear place for teaching as way of providing knowledge.

The second limitation is even more fundamental and applies to behaviour change more generally. It is this: if someone is ready to change, then staying focused on ambivalence is frustrating and counterproductive. If those you are working with have already bought into the idea of MI and want to become skilled, then dwelling for too long on why they might want to become skilled will be frustrating. They want to make changes. Let's get on with it! The same is true for the individual with a behaviour-change issue. If they want to change – they want to make a plan – staying focused for too long on whether and why they might want to change can be counterproductive. So, how to move beyond motivation in training?

Here we run into an uncomfortable fact: people do not become skilled after training in MI. There has been a fair bit of research and it is very consistent. A few days of training in MI is not enough to become skilled. In fact, this is not a finding that applies just to MI; it is widespread and raises questions about the purpose of training generally. Of course, people *do* become skilled at MI, but this happens in practice, not in training. Which begs the question: what is the point of training people in MI (or indeed other skills)?

Before answering that question, it is worth considering the possibility that the impact of training may actually be negative. This seems counterintuitive. Having spent a couple of days learning MI, surely participants come out with at least somewhat better practice and that must be a good thing? Unfortunately, that is not necessarily the case. Two days' training has been shown to have almost no impact on actual practice skills, but it has a very big impact on something else: self-assessed skills. In a nutshell, a two-day training course does not improve skills but makes people *think* that they are more skilled (Miller and Mount 2001). Miller has commented that he feels a two-day workshop on its own can often work as a way of 'inoculating' people against becoming good at MI. In the same way that a little bit of an illness provided through a vaccine can prevent the whole illness, so a little bit of training can make people feel that they know what they are doing – and therefore prevent them from feeling that they need to do anything more in order to be very skilled.

This is not a phenomenon confined to MI. In fact, this is a very well-evidenced phenomenon known as the Dunning–Kruger effect, in which a little bit of training or a little bit of knowledge increases confidence rapidly but competence very little (encapsulated in the phrase 'a little bit of knowledge is a dangerous thing'). In the diagram below, it is captured as 'Mount Stupid' – because people do not understand their lack of expertise. Then, as competence increases, we realise how little we know, and our confidence goes *down*. This is the 'Valley of Despair' – and as the name suggests, it is often the most challenging part of becoming skilful, as we are becoming less and less confident. This was, in fact, reflected in an unexpected finding from our first ever study of training in MI: the worse people were at MI, the better they rated themselves; conversely, the best workers tended to rate themselves as not being very good (Forrester *et al.* 2008c). However, if we stick with our commitment to becoming more skilled, we do regain confidence as well as competence, until we reach the 'Plateau of Sustainability'.

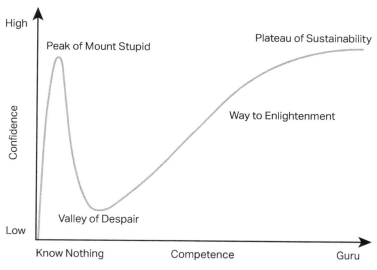

Figure 10.1   The Dunning–Kruger effect

The Dunning–Kruger effect has implications for how we support people to become good at MI. However, it is worth reflecting on whether it perhaps has more general implications for how we tend to support skills development in child and family work. How often – in practice, in training and in social work courses – do we give people a little bit of a method or a theory without providing the level of input required to help them become genuinely competent? Is there a possibility that we are accidentally inoculating people against becoming skilled in a wide variety of approaches? Certainly, our belief is that it is much better to become truly competent at a smaller number of things than to expect people to master a wide range of theories, methods and approaches (see Box 10.1).

So, in this context, what is the positive contribution that training can make to the development of competent MI practitioners? There are five key things that training can helpfully do. The five things and the order in which training should usually address them are:

1. *Build motivation and commitment.* As discussed above.

2. *Provide factual information.* In particular, it can outline the theories underpinning MI and it can summarise the evidence. Both of these are useful for those who want to become good at MI.

3. *Introduce key elements of practice.* Participants will not become skilled during training, but they may get some sort of understanding of key elements of MI in practice.

4. *Avoid complacency.* Prepare people for the fact that becoming truly competent is not an easy or straightforward process – ensuring that people are ready to move beyond their initial sense of feeling (overly) confident.

5. *Review progress.* Use the eight (or nine) stages for developing MI skills that we discussed in Chapter 9 to help people reflect on what progress they have already made, and what the next stages might be for them.

6. *Establish next steps and beyond.* Provide people with guidance on how they can further develop their expertise – the next steps that they can take on the journey to excellent practice. This is perhaps the most important contribution that training can make beyond building motivation.

HOW CAN WE DELIVER THESE ELEMENTS?

Training can take many forms – from a two-hour session through to many days – and the level and needs of the group will vary. It is not possible in the space we have to cover every eventuality. Here we want to introduce some basic principles for delivery.

Crucially, MI is not a closed resource. One of the things we like about MI is that it is developed and delivered by a community of curious practitioners, researchers and trainers. There is a downside to this: it is more difficult to ensure quality control. Some people say they are training people in MI but do not have the skills or knowledge to do this. However, this is compensated for by the fact that a wealth of resources is freely available online. We have mentioned motivationalinterviewing.org; this website provides access to a huge cache of resources for training – including the latest research, a store of great training exercises and links to videos and other information that may be useful. There are also many other resources, books and websites you can freely access. Here we make some general observations about how to train and the strengths and limitations of different types of training input.

A key axiom in MI is that people are more likely to be convinced by their own arguments than by those that you make for them – and much of MI is about how to facilitate people to convince themselves to change behaviour. In a similar way, people are more likely to learn and change through their own direct experiences, arguments and motivations. So good training offers limited formal teaching input and aims to skilfully structure sessions so that people can learn principles and practices for themselves.

In doing so, you might want to think about how to blend the following types of exercise together – and then find examples online:

- *Didactic teaching*

    Didactic teaching is the classic approach of standing up and telling people something. There is a need for this, but people take in notoriously little from what is sometimes called 'stand and deliver' teaching. To maximise the 'stickability' of didactic elements, we suggest three things. First, prepare the ground. If you have established a problem and are offering a solution, then people take things in much better. For instance, if you want to teach about the theory of change underlying MI, people are more likely to be receptive if they have just realised they do not have a theory of change for their current practice. Second, keep it short – and ideally fun. Third, provide an opportunity to put it into practice. This can be as simple as a small group discussion – but might also be any of the methods outlined here.

- *Little group, big group, cardboard box*

    The default of the tired trainer is to pose a question, discuss in small groups and then feed back into the main group. There is nothing wrong with this…provided it is used occasionally and for issues where this is likely to be helpful. The main problem is it can be a bit boring and predictable.

    It can be particularly powerful to do some exercises with the whole group together, particularly near the beginning and end of training sessions, as this can build group cohesion and shared values. For instance, we sometimes get the group to give us counselling using just reflections. Seeing how difficult this can be and understanding how powerful reflections are, while simultaneously getting to know the trainer much better than expected, is a powerful exercise.

- *Role plays*

  Often people say they do not like role plays. It is important to understand this reluctance – people may not like the possibility of showing up their own lack of skill in public. And some people do not like acting. Yet often when they give feedback, participants identify role plays as the key learning opportunity. Role plays have a number of potential advantages. You can set them up to represent the demands of your particular service or a particular type of challenge. You can design them to focus on learning a particular skill, or seeing what happens if a worker is deliberately bad. Because they are not real, they can be like laboratories to try specific skills.

  It is also important to emphasise that role plays can be simple or complicated, and short or long. Often a very focused one can provide better learning of a specific point than a much longer one. Where emotional issues are involved, do allow people to 'debrief' and get out of role – often it is a good idea to have a break after a role play.

- *Real plays*

  As the name suggests, a real play is intended to be a 'real' conversation undertaken in a 'playful' way. Unlike a role play, participants do not need to pretend to be anyone else. Instead, the idea is to identify a real issue that they are willing to talk about and then have a conversation in order to practise and develop MI skills. The issue you decide to talk about could be anything, such as quitting smoking, eating more healthily, taking more exercise or spending less time on screens. It does not really matter what the issue is, as long as it is genuine. Real plays are often more powerful than role plays in the early stages of skills development – because they provide opportunities to see how frustrating other approaches can be and how much better MI tends to be.

- *Other activities*

Often the best training sessions are characterised by variety. As well as having a set of small group and larger group activities, you can also think about some different activities to engage the attendees. We often find that groups of workers enjoy watching the trainers engage in role plays of their own, either demonstrating MI-adherent or non-MI-adherent approaches. You can then ask the group to take on the role of observer and provide feedback on the quality of the trainers' practice. There are also plenty of videos you can find on YouTube of people demonstrating MI skills in a range of different settings. Sometimes it is better to have a series of quick exercises to hand, to use throughout the day as needed, than a smaller set of long activities. There is a good list of these on the following website, which can be used free of charge for learning and training purposes: www.intrinsicchange.com/training-activities.html.

Other ways of supporting MI practice

Beyond training, it is really important to give people opportunities to reflect on their MI skills and to receive supportive feedback. As we discussed in Chapter 9, if we think about learning skills more generally, then most of our time is not going to be spent in formal lessons (training sessions). Most of the time we are going to need to practise. In this final section of the chapter, we consider how to use supervision and then how to provide feedback on observations of practice.

SUPERVISION

One of the key ways of supporting social workers in children's services more generally is through supervision (Ruch 2007). In that case, can supervision be used as a way of helping people develop their MI skills? And in what sense is a good supervisor like a good MI practitioner? It has been noted that the evidence base for supervision in social work is surprisingly absent (Carpenter *et al.* 2012). We do not know very much about how different approaches in supervision help to shape and influence what social workers do in practice. But there are some ideas about this that seem to us very likely to be true. The first is that the quality of your supervision and the kind of relationship you have with your supervisor is one important component of a well-functioning practice environment. Even if we might not know exactly what it means to provide high-quality supervision, we would be worried if a worker's experience of supervision was of a supervisor who found it hard to keep to scheduled meeting times, was rarely available for informal catch-ups, and when they did find time to meet with their supervisees, was only focused on adherence to process and showed no interest whatsoever in either their personal wellbeing or what positive difference they were making for children and families.

One suggestion for good supervision is that the supervisor should use the skills of MI with the worker. If by MI skills, this means listening well, respecting the worker's opinions, asking open questions, having a clear plan for the session, having a purposeful approach, and when there is disagreement, creating a dialogue, then we agree. These kinds of skills are very likely to be helpful in supervision. However, welcome as they may be, by themselves these skills are likely to have limited impact on the worker developing his or her MI competence. More directly then, could the supervisor use MI skills to explore the worker's ambivalence about what they should do, the kinds of decisions they should make, and listen out for change talk in response? We are not so sure. If we think about the kinds of decisions that a worker might need to make – should they recommend the case is closed, or kept open? Or what is their assessment about the level of harm to the child? These are not behaviour-change issues. The worker will not be feeling ambivalent about them in the same way they might in relation to their own practice and whether they want to develop MI skills.

In what other ways can supervision be used, then, to help workers develop their MI skills? The primary opportunity is to serve as a space for the worker to reflect on their practice, and to think about the extent to which they are able to demonstrate MI skills in practice and what else they need to do in order to become more MI-adherent. For example, it is quite common to hear in supervision the supervisor and worker agree a task, such as talking to the mother about the child's poor school attendance, or to the father about his use of cannabis. Often, this is where the discussion stops. The task has been agreed, the notes written on the file, and the focus moves on to the next child. But if we stop and think for a moment, the task that has just been agreed (to talk to a parent about an issue of concern) is actually very complicated. Typically, we suppose both that supervisors trust the worker's ability to complete the task without further input, and that if the worker felt they needed help, then they would ask. However, this does represent a missed opportunity to help the worker think about the conversation and, in particular, how they can use the skills of MI to maximise the likelihood of the session going well. Instead of moving on, we suggest that asking the worker some simple questions may help prompt them to reflect more carefully about the task, and come to see that it presents an opportunity for them to practise and demonstrate their MI skills. For example, the supervisor could ask:

- How are you going to introduce the topic to the parent?

- How clear are you about the purpose of the conversation, and how will you explain this to the parent?

- How do you think the parent will respond and what will you do if they demonstrate resistance?

- Why is it important for you to have this discussion with the parent?

As you will have noticed, all of these questions are *how* and *why* questions. And we think this is why they are potentially so helpful. In supervision, it is very common to hear discussions about *what* and *when* – what needs to be done and by when. It is much less common to hear discussions about how and why (Wilkins *et al.* 2017). But it is exactly these kinds of questions that prompt greater reflection and exploration. If the supervisor can use how and why questions, and link these to MI-related topics such as purpose, change talk and resistance, then we think there is real potential for supervision to help support the development of MI skills in workers.

OBSERVATION AND FEEDBACK

Despite all of the positive ways in which supervision can help workers to think about their practice and the extent to which they can use the skills of MI, it does not allow you to actually provide feedback on the quality of the worker's skills. Supervision sessions involve talking *about* practice. This is not to suggest that workers will mislead their supervisors, but as we saw when discussing the Dunning–Kruger effect, it is very hard for any of us to accurately describe our own capabilities. Either we will tend towards over-confidence or, just as problematic, under-confidence. It is also not possible to recount in detail what actually happened in any given session or meeting, not to the extent of who said what, the words they used and how the other person responded. Which is why in this section we want to emphasise the importance of observing social work practice directly and being able to give helpful feedback. We considered in the previous chapter how you might obtain audio-recordings of practice and how these could be used to support self-learning. Listening to someone else in an audio-recording and offering constructive feedback add another dimension to this. You can, of course, also observe someone in practice without audio-recording the session, much as practice educators (and others) observe student social workers. There is something important about being able to provide a second perspective, and especially when this can be combined with a good level of knowledge about MI.

In one of our projects, we worked over a long period of time with one local authority in England (Luckock *et al.* 2017). We collected many audio-recordings of social workers meeting with parents or young people, and then provided feedback to the workers in a coaching or feedback session. Feedback can be provided in a relatively open-ended way, in which you might discuss in general terms how the worker managed the meeting, how they talked about concerns or responded to disclosures, and the extent to which it felt like a helpful and productive session. Alternatively, you might choose to apply a coding framework to the recording, as discussed in Chapter 9. Whichever option you choose, it is important to think carefully about *how* to give feedback to the worker so that they feel motivated and empowered to continue developing their MI skills. This does not mean avoiding talking about any aspects of the recording that you find worrying or which involve the worker demonstrating non-MI-adherent skills, but it does mean taking a broadly strengths-based perspective and making sure that the worker understands that the purpose of the feedback is supportive, rather than critical. In previous chapters of the book, we considered in depth how to provide advice and how to have challenging conversations with parents, and the same principles would apply to difficult conversations with workers.

As an overall approach for providing feedback, the elicit–provide–elicit model is a helpful one. In Chapter 5, we considered how this model could be used by a worker in conversation with a parent. We suggested that in the first part of the discussion (elicit), the worker would ask open questions to find out what the parent already thinks about the issue, and reflections to show they are listening. In the next part (provide), the worker should note areas of agreement between themselves and the parent and demonstrate understanding of the parent's perspective (including areas of disagreement). Only then, using neutral language, should the worker provide information and advice, or share their own concerns. In the third part (elicit), the worker again asks open questions to explore what the parent now understands about the worker's point of view, and to ask what they think about what the worker has just said. We know that the same model can work well when giving feedback to workers about their practice (Figure 10.2, an adaptation of Figure 5.1). You can start by asking the worker open questions about the recording, and the aspects of the session that they think went well or less well (elicit). At this point, in our experience, many workers will be far more critical of their own practice than we might have been. If so, and you agree with them, then you can say so, while also being mindful to point out the strengths you noticed in the session too. If there are additional issues that you want to raise, you can then do this in the next part of the discussion (provide), ensuring that you use non-judgemental language. Finally, you can explore with the worker what they think about your feedback (elicit) and agree with them some next steps. For example, perhaps the worker is going to practise using more reflections or ask the parent to have more input into the agenda (depending on what the issues are that you have talked about).

Elicit	Provide	Elicit
• Ask mainly open questions about what the worker thinks about the audio-recording • Use reflections and summaries to show you have understood their point of view	• Agree with the worker's perspective wherever possible • Provide any new information or advice (or concerns you might have) • Use clear and neutral language • Avoid conveying personal judgement	• Acknowledge that more than one interpretation of the audio-recording is possible • Ask the worker to summarise what you have said • Ask for their perspective on the information or advice you have provided • Emphasise their autonomy and demonstrate empathy

Figure 10.2   The elicit–provide–elicit model for providing feedback

Conclusion

In this chapter, we have considered how MI itself gives us some insights into how we might support other people to develop their MI skills, and in particular the importance of engaging with people's values and motivations for change. We have looked at some ideas for training, while also emphasising that training by itself is insufficient. In fact, in discussing the Dunning–Kruger effect, we saw how a little bit of training may actually lead to over-confidence, rather than skill development. We then considered opportunities in supervision, observation and feedback to help people improve their practice.

It is hard to be prescriptive about the best way to support others, because we know that readers are likely to be in a whole range of different services, teams and roles. The key thing to take away is the importance of creating opportunities for reflection and practice combined with feedback (followed by more practice and more feedback).

Chapter 11

Concluding thoughts

In this final short chapter, we want to do two things. One is to outline what is not covered in this book, including being clear about what MI is *not*. This includes identifying gaps in our understanding of MI, thinking about some important criticisms and limitations, and suggesting future directions for research and practice. We then turn to consider what the contribution of MI is to child and family work, and why we believe it may be a particularly helpful approach.

What we did not cover – and why

There are several important areas not covered in this book. A particularly important one is assessment. This is a potential limitation, because assessment is such a central concern for children's services. We did not include a chapter on assessment because MI is a communication style. In theory, it says nothing about assessment; in practice, this is not the case, because assessment and communication are intertwined. In fact, a problem-saturated and risk-dominated approach to assessment is not consistent with MI. An MI-consistent approach requires more attention to strengths and identifying positives, while not ignoring risks and concerns. However, as MI was developed for counselling and communication, it does not have much to say about assessment as such. It is more that it assumes a strengths-orientated perspective as essential to helping people.

When we thought about what an MI-consistent approach to assessment would look like, we were particularly struck by the similarities between Signs of Safety and other solution-focused approaches and MI. To a large degree, they have done the work we would have done – and no doubt much better. Most importantly, they have considered how we can maintain a strengths- and solution-orientated perspective when we need to deal with risks and concerns. We felt that on balance it was more appropriate if we focused solely on the core strengths of MI, namely its lessons for communicating and helping people. In doing so, we hope that MI provides insights and suggestions that might complement and work well with various strengths-based approaches to risk assessment. We are aware of several really good books and online resources on strengths-based assessment (see 'Further resources' section). We would suggest that if you are interested in developing your thinking around MI, you explore some of these resources in thinking about how an MI communication style might be combined with a strengths-based approach to risk assessment.

A more substantive area that is missing is a focus on social factors. MI attends in detail to how to help individuals, how to have difficult conversations and how to help people address problem behaviours. It has little to say about broader structural issues, such as deprivation, race or gender. Yet we know these are crucial issues shaping the demand for services and the way we work with people (Featherstone *et al.* 2014). Indeed, an understanding and appreciation of these broader factors puts the 'social' into social work. The lack of attention to such issues is therefore a major gap in MI, and potentially the applicability of MI to children's social care situations.

This is not just a theoretical issue; it has major practical implications for how we work with people. Consider the real example of a conversation with a mother who has missed appointments to see her baby in foster care. When asked why, she says she did not have money for her bus fare. Should you have an MI-based conversation about the issue (helping her to explore how she might ensure she has enough money or exploring other options) or should you be ensuring she is given money or vouchers for the bus? The usual answer would probably be the latter, but our decision about what is right may be influenced by lots of factors. For instance, what if she *had* been given money for the bus, but says she spent it on food the night before? And what if you know she has a drug problem and suspect she actually spent the money on drugs?

We are not posing this conundrum because there is a 'right' answer, but because it highlights a theoretical limitation in MI and also offers us an insight into how we might address this limitation. The limitation is that because MI focuses on working with individuals, it may individualise problems or issues. It may make people responsible for decisions and changes that they should not be responsible for. Our response to this genuine issue has two elements.

First, as with any communication in child and family social work, how and when we should use MI needs to be guided by wise and thoughtful consideration of what we are doing and why we are doing it. MI provides detailed descriptions of how we can work with people, particularly around behaviour change or having difficult conversations. It does not answer the question about why we are having such conversations. To answer that, we need to be thoughtful, reflective professionals who think critically about the nature of the issues we are working with and how best to work with them. Communication cannot and should not be disconnected from such thinking.

Once we have done this, the second element of our response is that MI provides a good way of working within such thoughtful understandings of the work being undertaken. MI is inherently respectful and involves listening and understanding the perspective of the other person. As such, it is a really good place for starting conversations that take power and wider social structures seriously. This is not just an assertion we make based on our experience of MI: there is empirical evidence to support it. A summary of research studies found MI was particularly effective when working with black and minority people (Bahafzallah *et al.* 2020). A possible explanation for this is that the emphasis on understanding and valuing people's perspectives is particularly important in working with groups who have experienced oppression and discrimination. This is certainly our experience as practitioners and researchers and in training people. Put another way, MI can be thought of as a good description of key elements of the communication skills involved in anti-oppressive practice.

The importance of MI being guided by thoughtful, ethical and reflective thinking about what we are trying to achieve in our work with families is also central to a second challenge for MI. Is there a danger that MI might be manipulative? Would it not sometimes be more ethical to just say what you think people should do, rather than eliciting from them their 'intrinsic motivation'? Another way of framing this is that MI shares many characteristics with effective sales techniques. Even a cursory study of sales techniques highlights the importance of listening and building a relationship, of finding out what people want, of exploring the difference between what they currently have and what they might want, and of structuring the conversation to create action. These are very similar to core parts of MI. Is MI a way of manipulating people to do what you want them to do?

The honest answer is yes, it can be used in this way. MI has distilled many key insights into helping people to change behaviour. As such, it is potentially powerful stuff. For this reason, there is an emphasis within MI that it should always be informed by the 'spirit of MI'. The spirit of MI can be summarised as genuinely wanting the best for the other person. Like all methods we might use, how ethical they are is in large part defined by the purposes for which we are using them. The resolution to this is not that MI could not be used to manipulate people, but rather that we need to guard against the potential that it might be. In fact, this is probably true for any effective way of helping people change. If they tend to work, then they could be used unethically. The safeguard against this is not in the method; it is in the processes of ethical reflection that we engage in as professionals. Again, MI needs to be guided by thoughtful and ethical reflection to ensure we genuinely want the best for the people we are working with.

Considerations such as this are often discussed within the MI community, particularly in relation to whether MI is a specific method with skills that can be learnt or a 'way of being' that embodies key principles that apply to how to work with people and indeed how to be with people generally. Part of the reason for this difference is that when you are really helping people and have developed sufficient skill not to have to think about the skills you are using, there is a feeling of 'flow' and being in the moment, and a sense of connection and understanding. It may be that it does not matter whether you think of this as doing or being MI – it is probably more important that you have reached a level where you are very likely to be really helping people.

Future directions for MI

MI is a comparatively new approach within child and family social work, and there are many areas in which we need to know more. More research on the relationship between MI skills and outcomes for children and families, and on how to help practitioners to become more skilled, is needed. Yet many of the biggest questions are not primarily empirical but theoretical, such as how MI could embrace the social model or poverty-aware practice, or how MI can be combined with approaches such as

Signs of Safety or systemic practice. It would be particularly interesting to develop approaches to assessment and management of risk that incorporated the principles and practices of MI.

Why MI?

We started the book by identifying some of the key considerations that drew us to MI. It is worth briefly recapping these. We felt MI served as a corrective to a lot of current practice, which seemed rather authoritarian with little emphasis on respectful collaboration. MI provided useful ways of theorising resistance and understanding change and why it is so often difficult, but it simultaneously provided detailed guidance on the practice skills needed to help people. Finally, MI has a strong evidence base, which both reassures us that it is a good approach to use and allows us to understand its limitations.

There are other features of MI that appeal to us. It is 'open source' – it has not been trademarked or protected, and people are encouraged to try to use or adapt it. It is also relatively straightforward to understand. Systemic and psychodynamic approaches have offered much to social work, but they also tend towards the abstruse and complicated. We are drawn to an approach than can be explained and understood in relatively simple ways. We are probably all broadly humanist in orientation, with a fairly positive view of human nature, and MI fits well with this.

Yet while these are all rational and logical reasons for exploring the potential that MI has for improving our practice in child and family social work, they are not the real reason we have devoted so much time and effort to supporting people to use MI in this setting. For that, we need a different type of explanation. The real reason we are passionate about MI is that we have experienced directly the difference it can make. We have used it ourselves and seen the way in which it can make even very difficult conversations much more constructive. We have also seen the way workers experience learning MI as transformative; we have heard huge numbers of stories of how moving to an MI approach helped families and created real, meaningful and lasting changes. We have seen too the difference it makes in practice. Across hundreds of observations of practice, we have seen how MI approaches create better collaboration, minimise unnecessary confrontation and help people to make changes in their lives.

The magic of child and family social work happens when a worker meets a family and is able through their relationship with the family to help the child and carers. What keeps us all enthused and excited in this challenging profession are the times when that happens. For us, MI is the best description we know of how to make the magic happen. We hope that you will feel this book has given you enough to try MI out – and that when you do, you too feel the magic happen.

Further resources

The popularity of MI means there is a lot of information you can access with a bit of curiosity and a search engine of your choice. We would encourage you to go and have a look. Here we just collate a few good places to start.

Websites
The MINT website – Motivational Interviewing Network of Trainers (MINT)

This is a great resource, bringing together articles, video clips and much else. It is also a group that provides the best training on how to become a trainer – so it is well worth thinking about attending their sessions if possible.

> https://motivationalinterviewing.org

Intrinsic change

A website by a trainer which shares some great training activities that you can use on your own or if you are leading a session:

> www.intrinsicchange.com/training-activities.html

Steve Rollnick's website

One of the creators of MI, Steve delivers excellent training and shares his latest thoughts on this website:

> www.stephenrollnick.com

Books

The best book is the 'basic textbook', now in its third edition, and maybe a fourth will be out soon. It is:

Miller, W. R. and Rollnick, S. (2012) *Motivational Interviewing: Helping People Change.* New York, NY: Guilford Press.

There are many other books on the topic – Steve Rollnick's website links to applications in health, psychology, sport, education and others.

A particularly helpful one we have often used is:

Rosengren, D. B. (2017) *Building Motivational Interviewing Skills: A Practitioner Workbook.* New York, NY: Guilford Press.

It provides exercises you can do yourself or build into training or supervision – a great 'hands-on' resource.

A useful online resource on strengths-based assessment is:

Department of Health and Social Care (2019) *Strengths-based Approach: Practice Framework and Practice Handbook.* Available at https://assets. publishing.service.gov.uk/government/uploads/system/uploads/ attachment_data/file/778134/stengths-based-approach-practice-framework-and-handbook.pdf (accessed 20 January 2021).

References

Amrhein, P. C. *et al.* 2003. Client commitment language during motivational interviewing predicts drug use outcomes. *Journal of Consulting and Clinical Psychology 71*(5), 862–878.

Apodaca, T. R. *et al.* 2016. Which individual therapist behaviors elicit client change talk and sustain talk in motivational interviewing? *Journal of Substance Abuse Treatment 61*, 60–65.

Bahafzallah, L. *et al.* 2020. Motivational interviewing in ethnic populations. *Journal of Immigrant and Minority Health 22*, 816–851.

Bateson, G. 1972. *Steps to an Ecology of Mind: Collected Essays in Anthropology, Psychiatry, Evolution and Epistemology*. Chicago, IL: University of Chicago Press.

Bien, T. H. *et al.* 1993. Brief interventions for alcohol problems: A review. *Addiction 88*(3), 315–336.

Blom-Cooper, L. 1987. *A Child in Mind: The Report of the Panel of Inquiry into the Death of Kimberley Carlile*. London: London Borough of Greenwich.

Burman, S. 1997. The challenge of sobriety: Natural recovery without treatment and self-help groups. *Journal of Substance Abuse 9*, 41–61.

Carpenter, J. *et al.* 2012. Effective supervision in social work and social care. *SCIE Research Briefing 43*. Bristol: Social Care Institute for Excellence.

Clark, A. and Statham, J. 2005. Listening to young children: Experts in their own lives. *Adoption & Fostering 29*(1), 45–56.

Csikai, E. L. and Rozensky, C. 1997. 'Social work idealism' and students' perceived reasons for entering social work. *Journal of Social Work Education 33*(3), 529–538.

Curtis, K. *et al.* 2004. 'How come I don't get asked no questions?' Researching 'hard to reach' children and teenagers. *Child & Family Social Work 9*(2), 167–175.

Devaney, J. 2008. Chronic child abuse and domestic violence: Children and families with long-term and complex needs. *Child & Family Social Work 13*(4), 443–453.

Erikson, E. H. 1959. *Identity and the Life Cycle: Selected Papers*. New York, NY: International Universities Press.

Featherstone, B. *et al.* 2014. *Re-Imagining Child Protection: Towards Humane Social Work with Families*. Bristol: Policy Press.

Ferguson, H. 2005. Working with violence, the emotions and the psycho-social dynamics of child protection: Reflections on the Victoria Climbié case. *Social Work Education 24*(7), 781–795.

Ferguson, H. 2010. Walks, home visits and atmospheres: Risk and the everyday practices and mobilities of social work and child protection. *British Journal of Social Work 40*(4), 1100–1117.

Ferguson, H. 2011. *Child Protection Practice*. Basingstoke: Palgrave Macmillan.

Ferguson, H. 2017. How children become invisible in child protection work: Findings from research into day-to-day social work practice. *British Journal of Social Work* 47(4), 1007–1023.

Forrester, D. *et al.* 2008a. Evaluation of an intensive family preservation service for families affected by parental substance misuse. *Child Abuse Review: 17*(6), 410–426.

Forrester, D. *et al.* 2008b. Communication skills in child protection: How do social workers talk to parents? *Child & Family Social Work 13*(1), 41–51.

Forrester, D. *et al.* 2008c. Child risk and parental resistance: Can motivational interviewing improve the practice of child and family social workers in working with parental alcohol misuse? *British Journal of Social Work 38*(7), 1302–1319.

Forrester, D. *et al.* 2008d. How do child and family social workers talk to parents about child welfare concerns? *Child Abuse Review: 17*(1), 23–35.

Forrester, D. *et al.* 2013. *Reclaiming Social Work? An Evaluation of Systemic Units as an Approach to Delivering Children's Services.* Luton: University of Bedfordshire.

Forrester, D. *et al.* 2017. *Family Safeguarding Hertfordshire: Evaluation Report.* London: Department for Education.

Forrester, D. *et al.* 2018. A randomized controlled trial of training in Motivational Interviewing for child protection. *Children and Youth Services Review 88*, 180–190.

Forrester, D. *et al.* 2019. What is the relationship between worker skills and outcomes for families in child and family social work? *British Journal of Social Work 49*(8), 2148–2167.

Freud, S. 1923. *The Ego and the Id.* Vienna: Internationaler Psycho-analytischer Verlag/W. W. Norton & Company.

Galdston, I. 1955. Eros and Thanatos. *American Journal of Psychoanalysis 15*(2), 123–134.

Galvani, S. and Forrester, D. 2011. *Social Work Services and Recovery from Substance Misuse: A Review of the Evidence.* Edinburgh: Scottish Government.

Gibson, M. 2014. Social worker shame in child and family social work: Inadequacy, failure, and the struggle to practise humanely. *Journal of Social Work Practice 28*(4), 417–431.

Gibson, M. 2019. *Pride and Shame in Child and Family Social Work: Emotions and the Search for Humane Practice.* Bristol: Policy Press.

Glynn, L. H. and Moyers, T. B. 2010. Chasing change talk: The clinician's role in evoking client language about change. *Journal of Substance Abuse Treatment 39*(1), 65–70.

Gordon, T. 2008. *Parent Effectiveness Training: The Proven Program for Raising Responsible Children.* New York, NY: Harmony.

Grant, L. and Kinman, G. 2012. Enhancing wellbeing in social work students: Building resilience in the next generation. *Social Work Education 31*(5), 605–621.

Grassi, E. 2000. *Rhetoric as Philosophy: The Humanist Tradition.* Carbondale, IL: SIU Press.

Graybeal, C. 2001. Strengths-based social work assessment: Transforming the dominant paradigm. *Families in Society 82*(3), 233–242.

Greimel, K. V. and Kröner-Herwig, B. 2011. Cognitive behavioral treatment (CBT). In A. R. Møller *et al.* (eds) *Textbook of Tinnitus.* New York, NY: Springer, pp.557–561.

Group, P. M. R. 1993. Project MATCH (Matching Alcoholism Treatment to Client Heterogeneity): Rationale and methods for a multisite clinical trial matching patients to alcoholism treatment. *Alcoholism: Clinical & Experimental Research 17*(6), 1130–1145.

Group, P. M. R. 1997. Matching alcohol treatments to client heterogeneity: Posttreatment drinking outcomes, Part II. *Journal of Studies on Alcohol and Drugs 59*, 35–43.

Group, P. M. R. 1998. Matching patients with alcohol disorders to treatments: Clinical implications from Project MATCH. *Journal of Mental Health 7*(6), 589–602.

Hall, C. *et al.* 2013. Advice-giving. In Hall, C. *et al.* (eds) *Analysing Social Work Communication: Discourse in Practice.* Abingdon: Routledge, pp.89–116.

Hall, C. and White, S. 2005. *Looking Inside Professional Practice: Discourse, Narrative and Ethnographic Approaches to Social Work and Counselling.* Thousand Oaks, CA: SAGE.

Harwin, J. *et al.* 2014. *Changing Lifestyles, Keeping Children Safe: An Evaluation of the First Family Drug and Alcohol Court (FDAC) in Care Proceedings.* London: Brunel University.

Kant, I. 1998. *Critique of Pure Reason.* Cambridge: Cambridge University Press.

Kinman, G. and Grant, L. 2010. Exploring stress resilience in trainee social workers: The role of emotional and social competencies. *British Journal of Social Work* 41(2), 261–275.

Lefevre, M. 2010. *Communicating with Children and Young People: Making a Difference.* Bristol: Policy Press.

Lefevre, M. *et al.* 2017. Building trust with children and young people at risk of child sexual exploitation: The professional challenge. *British Journal of Social Work* 47(8), 2456–2473.

Luckock, B. *et al.* 2017. *The Islington 'Doing What Counts: Measuring What Matters' Evaluation Report.* London: Department for Education.

Lundahl, B. W. *et al.* 2010. A meta-analysis of motivational interviewing: Twenty-five years of empirical studies. *Research on Social Work Practice* 20(2), 137–160.

Lynch, A. *et al.* 2019. What does empathy sound like in social work communication? A mixed-methods study of empathy in child protection social work practice. *Child & Family Social Work* 24(1), 139–147.

Magill, M. *et al.* 2018. A meta-analysis of motivational interviewing process: Technical, relational, and conditional process models of change. *Journal of Consulting and Clinical Psychology* 86(2), 140.

Manuel, J. *et al.* (eds) 2012. *Motivational Interviewing: A Review of Coding Systems.* Poster presented at the Motivational Interviewing Network of Trainers (MINT) Forum, Fort Wayne, IN.

Maslow, A. H. 1954. The instinctoid nature of basic needs. *Journal of Personality* 22(3), 326–347.

Messer, S. B. and Wampold, B. E. 2002. Let's face facts: Common factors are more potent than specific therapy ingredients. *Clinical Psychology: Science and Practice* 9(1), 21–25.

Miller, W. R. 1983. Motivational interviewing with problem drinkers. *Behavioural and Cognitive Psychotherapy* 11(2), 147–172.

Miller, W. R. *et al.* 2001. Enhancing motivation for change in problem drinking: A controlled comparison of two therapist styles. *Journal of Consulting and Clinical Psychology* 61(3), 455–461.

Miller, W. R. and Mount, K. A. 2001. A small study of training in motivational interviewing: Does one workshop change clinician and client behavior? *Behavioural and Cognitive Psychotherapy* 29(4), 457.

Miller, W. R. and Moyers, T. B. 2006. Eight stages in learning motivational interviewing. *Journal of Teaching in the Addictions* 5(1), 3–17.

Miller, W. R. and Moyers, T. B. 2017. Motivational interviewing and the clinical science of Carl Rogers. *Journal of Consulting and Clinical Psychology* 85(8), 757.

Miller, W. R. and Rollnick, S. 2013. *Motivational Interviewing: Helping People Change (Applications of Motivational Interviewing).* New York, NY: Guilford Press.

Miller, W. R. and Rose, G. S. 2009. Toward a theory of motivational interviewing. *American Psychologist* 64(6), 527.

Moyers, T. *et al.* 2014. *Motivational Interviewing Treatment Integrity Coding Manual 4.1 (MITI 4.1).* Unpublished manual.

Moyers, T. B. *et al.* 2016. The Motivational Interviewing Treatment Integrity code (MITI 4): Rationale, preliminary reliability and validity. *Journal of Substance Abuse Treatment* 65, 36–42.

Musser, P. H. et al. 2008. Motivational interviewing as a pregroup intervention for partner-violent men. *Violence and Victims* 23(5), 539–557.

Nelsen, J. C. 1975. Dealing with resistance in social work practice. *Social Casework* 56(10), 587–592.

O'Connell, B. 2012. *Solution-Focused Therapy* (3rd edition). London: SAGE.

Patterson, G. and Forgatch, M. (eds) 2001. *Therapist Behavior as a Determinant for Client Noncompliance: A Paradox for the Behavior Modifier*. Annual Meeting of the American Psychological Association, July 1982, Washington, DC. Washington, DC: American Psychological Association.

Plant, R. 2009. *Social and Moral Theory in Casework* (Routledge Revivals). Abingdon: Routledge.

Proschaska, J. and DiClements, C. 1984. *The Transtheoretical Approach: Towards a Systematic Eclectic Framework*. Homewood, IL: Dow Jones Irwin.

Randall, C. L. and McNeil, D. W. 2017. Motivational interviewing as an adjunct to cognitive behavior therapy for anxiety disorders: A critical review of the literature. *Cognitive and Behavioral Practice* 24(3), 296–311.

Reid, W. J. and Shapiro, B. L. 1969. Client reactions to advice. *Social Service Review* 43(2), 165–173.

Rogers, C. R. 1951. *Client-Centered Counseling*. Boston, MA: Houghton-Mifflin.

Rollnick, S. *et al.* 2005. Consultations about changing behaviour. *British Medical Journal* 331(7522), 961–963.

Rollnick, S. *et al.* 2016. *Motivational Interviewing in Schools: Conversations to Improve Behavior and Learning*. New York, NY: Guilford Press.

Ruch, G. 2007. 'Thoughtful' practice: Child care social work and the role of case discussion. *Child & Family Social Work* 12(4), 370–379.

Ruch, G. 2012. Where have all the feelings gone? Developing reflective and relationship-based management in child-care social work. *British Journal of Social Work* 42(7), 1315–1332.

Schön, D. A. 1983. *The Reflective Practitioner*. New York, NY: Basic Books.

Strait, G. *et al.* (2012) Using motivational interviewing with children and adolescents: A cognitive and neurodevelopmental perspective. *Advances in School Mental Health Promotion* 5(4), 290–304.

Team, U. R. 2005. Effectiveness of treatment for alcohol problems: Findings of the randomised UK alcohol treatment trial (UKATT). *British Medical Journal* 331(7516), 541.

Turnell, A. and Edwards, S. 1999. *Signs of Safety: A Solution and Safety Oriented Approach to Child Protection Casework*. New York, NY: W. W. Norton & Company.

Wilkins, D. *et al.* 2017. What happens in child and family social work supervision? *Child & Family Social Work* 22(2), 942–951.

Wozniak, R. H. 1993. *Theoretical Roots of Early Behaviourism: Functionalism, the Critique of Introspection, and the Nature and Evolution of Consciousness*. London: Routledge/Thoemmes/Kinokuniya Co.

Zhang, S. *et al.* 2019. The impacts of family treatment drug court on child welfare core outcomes: A meta-analysis. *Child Abuse & Neglect* 88, 1–14.

Subject Index

Author Index